7-95

To Paula + David

New Life
for Dying Churches

It Can Happen Anywhere

May His love
make it happen
wherever you go.
God Bless,

New Life
for Dying Churches

It Can Happen Anywhere

by
Rose Sims

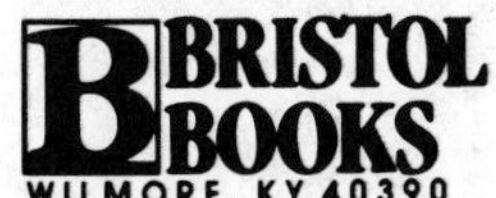

NEW LIFE FOR DYING CHURCHES
It Can Happen Anywhere

Published by Bristol Books

First Edition, September 1989

Scripture quotations indicated (KJV) are from the King James Bible.

Library of Congress Card Number: 89-61121
ISBN: 0-917851-38-2
Suggested Subject Headings:
1. Church Renewal
2. Church Growth
Recommended Dewey Decimal Classification: 262.0017

BRISTOL BOOKS
An Imprint of Good News, a Forum for Scriptural Christianity, Inc.
308 East Main Street • Wilmore, KY 40390

Contents

Foreword

A raucous loudspeaker is playing the National Anthem and nobody is standing at attention. Old Glory is exploding in a hundred red, white and blue spangles during the July 4, 1988, finale of the largest fireworks display east of the Mississippi, but nobody is saluting.

In a moment of bitter truth, I have to admit, "it is my fault. . . . I can't blame the Communists, the Democrats, the youth or the politicians. I let it happen in my generation."

My parents handed me a country with pure air, crystal clear streams and good earth undefiled by toxic and nuclear waste. My generation bled and died to save the world from Hitler and Hirohito, making it free for democracy. My husband, Jim Sims, came home from World War II to bands playing "America the Beautiful" and "The Church in the Wildwood."

Then I stood by and let it happen with such suddenness that I wonder if we are near the point of no return.

If so, then all I can hand our grandchildren is water so polluted we dare not eat its fish, an earth so fouled with chemical and nuclear waste we dare not eat its fruit. We are besieged with cancer, AIDS and a thousand other plagues which baffle our medical and technical experts. Our air, with its damaged ozone layer, threatens to choke to death generations yet unborn.

But far more ominous is the intellectual erosion which I, as a teacher of teachers, must in near defeat confess has caused grade scores to plummet until our best colleges reject even our brightest valedictorians. Illiteracy has clouded the dreams of a nation whose citizens' average reading scores hover near primary school level. More astounding is the way myriads of strong young minds are dying from experimentation with self-destructive drugs. Hundreds of teenage parents are dropping out of school and an alarming number of babies are born already drug addicted. Child abuse, sex abuse, the alarming divorce rate, crime and violence stalks every village. And my generation allowed it to happen.

But the final and perhaps fatal blow to our "one nation under God" is the loss of the church as a fulcrum in our daily lives. The church in America is an endangered species, powerless when it is most needed. The clergy—and I am one—are uniquely responsible.

This nation, established and abundantly blessed by God, is racing ever farther from its point of origin. Peter Marshall, in *The Light and the Glory*, has said,

> On a transatlantic airliner, as the navigator plots the plane's projected course, at a certain point he will make a neat dot and circle it, and label it PNR. Once that point is passed, for the plane to go back to its point of departure would require more fuel than remains on board. The plane has just passed the POINT OF NO RETURN. America has not quite reached that point . . . yet.

None of us can save the whole world, but with God's help each of us can save our little corner. One person and God are still a majority, and each of us must remember that, as Truman said, "the buck stops here." When we do, we can make "one nation under God" happen anywhere and everywhere. To that end, this circuit riding grandmother has written this account of how Christ and his power offer a chance for a change *now*, before we reach the point of no return.

It is crucial that the clergy in the pulpit again proclaim, "if my people, who are called by my name, will humble themselves and pray and seek my face and turn from their wicked ways, then I will hear from heaven and will forgive their sin and will heal their land" (2 Chronicles 7:14).

Rose Sims
Trilby United Methodist Church
Dade City, Florida 34297-0631

1

Songs in the Night

Eleanor Roosevelt once said, "I have never wanted to be a man. I have always wanted to excel. I have never thought it took a pair of trousers to do that." Eleanor's classic remark was not meant to discredit the man on whose ladder she climbed to reach her star. Rather she wanted to engender in women the vision of a day when each mortal could be judged on the basis of his or her own merits, capabilities and unique God-given talents.

At my conception, if God had asked me, "boy or girl?" I would, knowing what I know now, have answered a resounding, "girl." I love being a woman and I love men . . . good strong men who are so secure in their manhood that they allow their women to be all God intends them to be. Throughout my life, as I have stood at various crossroads, such men have stood beside me, cheering me on. What a joy they have made of my journey.

First was my father, a Danish pioneer immigrant and a sterling Christian visionary. Ahead of his time, he dared to come to this new, raw country. Unschooled in English, he went to college, plowed virgin land and died building the Alcan Highway that paved the way for Alaska's statehood.

Then, like a refreshing, sturdy March wind, Rev. Koch, a writer, lecturer and pioneer Danish Lutheran pastor, opened his home and his heart to me as a little girl. He initiated my soul to the world of Kirkegaard, Gruntvig, Bach and Hayden . . . and the little country church.

By the time I was twelve, Rev. Emil Nielsen, a Baptist country preacher who lived his life joyfully in total faith in an obscure corner of God's kingdom, became my hero. During the Great Depression, the Nielsens shared their home with me. Much later, I learned that their main salary was the chickens, vegetables and eggs delivered lovingly to the parsonage door by rough, country-hewn men who were fulfilling the biblical edict to give of what they had. In Rev. Nielsen's little country church I gave my heart and life to Christ. There I learned that I was a sinner lost and undone, that heaven is a free gift, that God is love, but he also must be our judge, and that he sent his only begotten Son so that whoever in faith believes and receives has eternal life.

It was there that my love affair with the country church began. It would span forty-five years and would be blended with three of the finest men God ever gave one woman to love. This love was to encompass laughter and tears, dark valleys of grief and shimmering mountaintops of transfiguration which only faith can climb.

On a sultry summer evening in 1944, while distant guns roared on the Normandy shores, I said a resounding and jubilant "I do" to a lanky, proud Viking immigrant ministerial student. Little did I know that Oscar's lifelong love affair was to be with me . . . and the vanishing country churches of his adopted America.

Like Peter of old who stood washing his empty nets, this brilliant Norseman, born on the windswept coastal fishing island of Mosterhavn, Norway, heard the call to fish for men. Laying down his nets and leaving all, he bought the last ticket on the last ship going to America just as the Nazis stormed his homeland.

He arrived in Chicago with seven dollars and a scholarship to attend Northern Baptist Seminary, and he promptly got a job as a bus boy at Marshall Field's department store. He failed every course the first semester while he carefully learned enough English so that he never again would fail a course—not through seminary, college, or the finest graduate schools of his adopted land. For twenty-seven years he charted his pilgrimage from one country church to another. Through the turbulent gales that batter and too often sink frail, faltering country churches, he weathered every storm to bring countless dying churches into a safe harbor. Burning with Wesley's dream of a church at every crossroad, Oscar deplored the statistics which told how each day, like ships that go down at sea, one of these churches disappears. Unable to stay afloat, victims of broken dreams or conflict, and abandoned or with an unskilled crew, silent as ghost ships sailing without captains they vanish on the horizon.

His heart ached for the churches of his adopted land. Why, without wake or weeping, were churches which had given birth to so many of America's great and small—bishops and bakers, presidents and paupers, ministers and miners—dying? How could denominations with millions of dollars and a God who said nothing was impossible let one church after another die? Weren't these churches built by the immigrants and pioneers who forged westward amid summer droughts, winter blizzards, disease and death, with but one vision—to plant their faith on the lonely frontier of a young and struggling democracy?

Loving Oscar as I did, it was easy to share his dream. Through the years, I learned that it meant standing alone together, opening church doors shut as tightly as great coffin lids, after the mourners had gone home. "That church is dead," they would say. "It was best it closed." And then they would give a hundred reasons, not one of which made sense to this Norseman who always came home at sunset with his boat filled to sinking with fish.

Time and again, three years after Oscar had stood at a tightly barred door, that church would lead the state in professions of faith and missions. Lives were miraculously changed by his undaunted faith in the Master Builder.

Then, because churches of the quality he forged were always in demand, a full-time pastor would be appointed. Once again we would be standing at a lonely, nearly forgotten, nailed-shut church door. Time after time, over twenty-seven years, Oscar proved that renewal could happen anywhere fishermen dared to battle the elements of neglect and discouragement and put out their nets for a catch.

One cannot sleep with such a giant of the faith, bear his children, share his ministry and message and witness people being born into the kingdom without catching the vision. Gladly would I have followed him to the ends of the earth, serving by his side, turning his parsonages into homes, singing in his choirs, teaching his Sunday schools, organizing his women's groups and praying and laughing and loving my way through a hundred closed churches. Such was my love. Such was the faith he taught by precept and example.

Strong men produce strong women. Oscar believed in me. Though my high school grades were dismal, he felt I was wise. As I worked at menial tasks to put him through school—waiting tables, scrubbing floors—he encouraged me to read his books. At night he tutored me in what he had learned. Could we have afforded it, I would have attended his classes. I typed his assignments from the first paper to his dissertation. Finally, our children grown, he insisted it was my turn. With a seven hundred dollar a month tax-free scholarship in hand, I had my day in the sun.

In 1971, after years of taking a course here and a course there, I became one of the few women past the age of forty-five to earn a doctorate, finishing my doctoral course work in one year. I, who had barely made it through high school, stood that August day on our twenty-seventh wedding anniversary graduating with a Doctor of Education in counseling, psychology and education.

I had watched Oscar receive four degrees. Our oldest child was about to get her M.D. from the University of Louisville Medical School. Our second born had earned her M.S. in music from the Cincinnati Conservatory of Music. Our daughter Lee was finishing at the University of Missouri. Now it was indeed my turn. I became Dr. Rose, as I was to be called for many years as I served little churches, taught on university campuses, did research in the Orient and Europe and studied as a visiting scholar at Harvard.

Now we could both teach and work in campus ministry and spend weekends opening closed country churches. Life was indeed beautiful that spring of 1971.

We had just finished a wonderful year of teaching at Hannibal LaGrange College in Hannibal, Missouri. With our possessions in storage, we turned in our grades and said goodbye to a vital weekend country church. We planned to spend a summer in Norway before beginning a new teaching career at Central Methodist College in Fayette, Missouri. True to form, along with his teaching assignment, Oscar had accepted the challenge of opening nearby New Hope United Methodist Church.

Little did I know as we flew to Norway that magnificent June morning that soon Oscar's mantle would fall upon my reluctant, grief-bent shoulders. Nor did I suspect that this journey would be his farewell to his beloved fjords and fatherland.

However, a second sense told me he was not well. *Surely not now, God!* I prayed. *Not just now when we were free to really open country churches!* We had stood just five years before in the great Cobo Hall in Detroit and heard Oscar declared the "Outstanding Rural Minister in America" for the American Baptist Convention. The Rosa O. Hall Award hung on the study wall. Coming South, we had become Methodists. There had been such a need, and church officials seemed convinced of his dream. For the first time the church hierarchy was believing that with the right leadership and backing from church leaders, dwindling churches could be injected with new life and vitality in a nation in crisis which so desperately needed what they had to offer.

We wanted to spend the rest of our days writing and teaching America how to preserve its most precious asset—the faith, fellowship and fervor found at the old altars where countless country folks had knelt to be born anew.

Half of all Protestant churches had fewer than fifty people in church on any given Sunday. Four thousand Methodist churches had closed since 1965. Hundreds of others needed new courage and the Wesley vision. Surely, having proven that tiny, faltering churches can come alive, nobody would write off our vision as mere theory. Oscar's dream now had the substance of reality. It was its best hour. Back to basics in education . . . back to basics in faith—the fellowship of believers, the Aldersgate experience of newness in Jesus Christ.

Yes, the future was before us. I was glad for every heartache we had shared, every church we had struggled to birth, all of the laughter which had rung through a dozen dilapidated parsonages and the faith it had spawned in me. I didn't know how much I would draw on that faith in the dark days ahead.

But on that June morning of 1971, Norway bound, all I could think of was the faith Oscar and his God had buried deep in my heart. Memories of country gospel sings, eatin' meetin's, revivals and rebirths flooded my soul. How rich we were, how good life was. Spring was never more beautiful. The robin had returned early and was singing in our apple tree. Oscar had finally received full conference membership, and we were headed for two wonderful months in Europe.

We visited Oscar's windswept native island, Mosterhavn, Norway. Then by Eurail pass we explored the homeland of my parents, who had immigrated to America in 1909. I stood in the pulpit of Kongenskirke, the ancient cathedral where my great grandfather had preached for so many years to the King of Denmark. My parents had met on the ship on their way to America. Knowing very little English, Dad enrolled in Dana College in Blair, Nebraska, and Mother earned her R.N. at Douglas County Hospital's School of Nursing in Omaha, Nebraska. Marriage and nine children had followed.

On a sun-drenched summer afternoon, just after we returned from Europe, with the Queen Anne's lace bedecking every country roadside and the meadow lark belting his heart out, I learned that the light of my life was going out. Oscar had Lou Gehrig's disease. In four months he would die. I heard the doctor say it loud and clear. My head told me it was the truth. But my heart told me it was a cruel lie. The meadow lark still sang lustily in the lilac tree, but I didn't hear the song. Gone forever were the mornings of love and laughter, of waking to hear children on Main Street playing "Run Sheep Run," of knowing that we were a vital part of making God come alive to a congregation of stalwart, genuine country giants. I recalled with pain the gentle way Oscar's love and faith in me had made me stretch to reach those mountain tops he believed I could climb.

Death has its own kinds of paranoia for those who are spectators. We want someone to do something for us, to stop time and let us catch our breath and ask if there isn't some other time, much, much farther down the road, when we would be stronger and better able to make the real unreal. At a time like this how could Oscar pragmatically ask me to forget myself and remember the call. "No, Oscar, I can't serve New Hope," I told him. He insisted. He asked me to help the struggling church until he could get well. I clung to hope. Maybe God would heal. *I'll strike a bargain with you, God,* I prayed. *I'll preach if you will make him well.*

All of his life, Oscar had fought to keep the country church alive. Without fail, wherever Oscar undertook the seemingly hopeless task of bringing a forlorn, unpainted, locked up church to life, in a few short months an electric spirit of hope was born. All those years he had beaten the odds, confounding every church growth planner's grim predictions, every pessimist who said it couldn't be done. Now he was dying, and more country churches were dying than when he had begun. What did he have to show for the time, the sacrifice? Everywhere he had planted beautiful buildings and vital congregations. Many had survived, some had not. Maybe those people whose hopes had been raised, only to be dashed, were worse off than if he had never come.

I expected his first thought when he learned he was terminally ill would be, "Rose, what will happen to us?" Instead it was, "Rose, what will happen to New Hope? Would you go out and preach? Hold the church for me. Maybe we can lick this thing . . . pray for a miracle." While I was deep in pain and self pity, as always, he was ten steps ahead, searching for God's will even in death.

But New Hope Church was not my only challenge. Enroute home from Europe, we had scheduled two weeks at a seminar at Philander Smith College in Little Rock, Arkansas. It was there, in an unfamiliar hospital, far from friends, that I learned of Oscar's impending death. I never should have called the college in Missouri to tell them Oscar was ill and could not teach. Our landlord heard the news, and rented our house to someone else. I also learned that while we had been in Europe, the mighty Mississippi had flooded its banks and swept Hannibal in its wake. Everything we owned was lost in the flood. The final blow came when the Little Rock hospital told me it did not care for terminally ill patients and Oscar must be discharged at once.

I felt I had to talk with someone . . . a minister or counselor. I, who had been director of counseling and head of the Psychology Department at Hannibal LaGrange College, needed counsel. What should I tell Oscar? The children? How should I tell them? Where would I find a house? How could I teach if no hospitals would care for a terminally ill spouse? How would I support the family?

I had six hours until I had to pick up Ron and Rob, our adopted sons, from day care. In a daze, I stumbled out of the doctor's office and into six downtown churches, one after another. "Is the pastor in?" I asked. "Do you have an appointment?" the secretary would ask. "Can you come back tomorrow?" This experience taught me a lesson: People in crisis can't phone ahead for an appointment.

At six o'clock I picked up the children, saw a theater marquee that read "Pinocchio," and bought two tickets for the boys. When they were settled watching the movie, I went to a pay phone to call New York and tell the girls their father was dying. The next morning I dialed the operator and asked for any doctor listed in the Fayette yellow pages. God did the picking. I breathed a prayer of thanks when an eighty-year-old M.D. whose kindly bedside manner came from his deep Christian compassion answered my call. "Bless your heart, my dear. We have just built a new wing to our hospital, and I will see he has a bed as long as he needs one."

A call to the college put me in touch with Miss Potter, a nearly eighty-year-old secretary who had given her life to the college and still worked in her office until midnight. She and God found a house directly behind my classroom. It had ten rooms and was only eighty dollars a month. Renting two rooms to college students would pay half my rent.

We put Oscar in the back of the station wagon and headed for Fayette, Missouri. The dark night of the soul is lighted with love. All night long I remembered a verse I had lived by through other dark hours: "I will trust and not be afraid. The Lord is my strength and my song; he has become my salvation" (Isaiah 12:2). Truly he does give songs in the night.

2

A Bargain with God

Children never forget their first day of school. I shall always remember my first Sunday in ministry.

It was not my first trip to New Hope. Oscar and I had looked the church over the previous March when we had signed a contract at Central Methodist College. Now it was August. I remembered how the church had looked last spring. The roof had a hole where raccoons had come in out of the cold. The door was sagging and the peeling clapboards pleaded for paint. Pencil in hand, Oscar had sketched his vision on a brown paper sack . . . new roof, enlarge this, paint that, pews, an educational unit here. Then we would need a kitchen and rest rooms and a new foyer. I had always dreamed with him. I hardly needed faith when he was beside me, for he had made it happen so many times.

But now I stood alone. My doctorate in psychology, counseling and education hardly made me a theologian. Many long years ago I had attended four years at the Northwestern Bible School and Seminary and earned a Bachelor of Religious Education. Aside from that, I also had some credits at Northern Baptist Seminary, a Bachelor of Science in Education, Master of Education in Counseling and Psychology, Specialist in Education of the Disadvantaged and my Doctor of Education.

But none of those credentials seemed nearly as important as the fact that for twenty-seven years, while standing beside Oscar, I had witnessed miracle after miracle in one seemingly dead church after another. I learned to believe that all things are possible with God. But that was when I had Oscar by my side to carry out the dream.

I had always been his support system, his prayer partner, holding the hammer and nails for him while he drafted and designed for God. Now on this grim day I realized he could not lead the way. What kind of courage did it take for him to hand the reigns over to me? "Maybe I will get well. Take it until I do." Was he also bargaining with God? Did I have faith to believe he could beat the odds? Did I have to take up the gauntlet to prove it to him?

That first Sunday at New Hope I preached my only sermon. Years before, Oscar had become violently ill with flu just as the service was beginning. He called me out of the choir and asked me to preach for him. Someone had told me when I became a pastor's wife that I must be ready to preach, pray and move on a moment's notice. Well, I had had the moment's notice. The choir was already filing in. I had no time to think. I opened my mouth and asked God to fill it.

Standing in the pulpit I opened my Bible and began reading. "To one man he gave five talents of money, to another two talents, and to another one talent" (Matthew 25:15). That scripture had always seemed like God's arithmetic . . . use it and it multiplies, waste it and it subtracts.

Except for that one dusty sermon, my barrel was empty. But for now, that was enough. *Let me get through this one awful day,* I prayed.

Then the miracle happened that was to happen so many, many times after that. As I was speaking for God, in his place, I found myself pouring out my heart to my self. What did it matter that the church was nearly empty? I needed that sermon.

After what seemed an eternity the sermon was over. Wrestling with myself, I told God, "No way can I be a women clergy. If I can't be a minister's wife any more, let me hear your 'well done' and let us both go out in a blaze of glory."

Before me stretched a new and challenging professorate. The

only woman on staff with a doctorate, I had to make good. I could serve him there. Today would be my final farewell to country churches. God would understand and so should Oscar. I could not serve on Oscar's call.

They were singing the last hymn. "My Hope Is Built ." This was the swan song. Oscar was dying . . . his ministry was finished. Tears filled my eyes. I had to get out. I would serve God however, wherever he wanted me, but I would not be a woman minister. *Not now, not ever. No, God! Please! God let me go home to the hospital to explain this to Oscar.* Nobody had ever understood me like Oscar. Oscar, my best friend, my confidant.

I looked for an escape route. *Dear God, I can't face the people crying. Let me take my children and flee out the closest exit.* I never liked goodbyes. Now I was saying goodbye to country churches, and the ultimate goodbye . . . to Oscar. I would explain all this to God on the long forty miles back to campus. Plenty of men would agree with me. Women just aren't cut out to be preachers. I meant it, and I was sure I was in God's will. No loving God could ask me to preach when I had a new job, a sick husband, three kids in college, and was having to be both parents at once to two young boys.

The benediction was finished. I spied the door behind the pulpit. Let someone else shake hands and explain what seemed to me to be obvious . . . men belong in pulpits, wives are supposed to be helpmates. That's scriptural and that's final, I assured myself. Then, like Lot's wife, I looked back.

There, taking his father's usual place at the door, stood my nine-year-old adopted son, shaking hands with the congregation. A victim of neglect, he had lived in fourteen foster homes before he came to us. His parents were in prison, he knew his father was dying—but there he stood shaking hands at the church door.

I wish I could say I heard a clarion call, a celestial voice, or had a vision. But I only saw four-feet six-inches of a nine year old, standing there alone, while I was busy trying to flee. Moses, when resisting God's call, could not have had a more convincing revelation. Like Moses, I knew at that moment what I had to do.

Years later, a student sat in my office and asked about "the call." He had been asked to serve a closed church near the college but he was "waitin' for a call. I'd go out there if I only knew I had a call." He asked me how I knew I had a call.

I told him about a Christmas Eve morning at six a.m. when we were stranded by a blinding snowstorm at a Holiday Inn in Kirksville, Missouri. We had been waiting for a waitress for some time. The dining room was filling up with irate customers, eager to be served and on their way. A young student was cooking in the kitchen. Neither waitresses, cashier nor hostess had been able to brave the storm. I listened to the blizzard howling outside and the storm brewing inside and remembered that I had worked my way through school as a waitress. A very good one, in fact. God never gives us an experience for no reason. I found out what my family wanted to eat, wrote it down and went to the kitchen and asked the student if he would fix it. I told him I had been a waitress and asked him if he needed help.

He gave me a pad and pencil, and soon I had everyone's order. When some complained about not getting coffee fast enough, I divulged the secret that I was a customer. What had been bedlam became family. Some people helped me serve. Others poured coffee. Each person wrote out his own check. Someone began singing carols. And I shared my faith. By the time the wind abated and the roads cleared enough for the manager to arrive, we all seemed like fast friends.

I asked my student, "Was I called to be a waitress that morning?" He pondered the question. "Maybe," I continued, "When there is a need, when you know how to fill it, when nobody else is going to do it, God is calling *you*."

Yes, there was an obvious need at New Hope. I was able to fill it. Nobody else would. Looking back at God's blessings over my seventeen years in the ministry, I have to thank God for that call.

I returned to New Hope the next Sunday and the next. Summer turned to autumn. Each Sunday, amid the blaze of flamboyant red, gold and yellow, I filled the melancholy moments of mellow Indian summer mornings with ministry.

God, don't let the leaves fall, I prayed. *Twenty-seven years of love and laughter is not enough. Let me hold this autumn in my heart a little longer.* I took the boys trick or treating. We had a Halloween Costume party at the church. I brought out a carload of college students dressed as ghosts, witches, even an owl. Ron, Rob and I went as the pumpkin family, stopping by the hospital to show

Oscar. Would this be his last Halloween? I remembered how he took the girls trick or treating long ago.

I established a routine. Up early. Prayer time., study my lectures, grade papers, a quick trip to the hospital, get the boys off to school, sing all the way to the office. By then the courage returned. Teach, eat lunch at the hospital, supervise student teachers council, launch the boys on their paper routes, then all of us to the hospital, home, empty bed. *God, stop the clock; just another year, another half-year.*

By Thanksgiving Oscar was in a coma. Now I began bargaining with God that I would preach if only Oscar could be alive. "Let him be a vegetable if you have to," I begged, "but don't let him leave me."

A gentle, mild winter came to Missouri. The campus was garlanded with gold and green, and the college chorale sang "For the Lord God Omnipotent Reigneth, Hallelujah." Amidst the glow of students going home for the holidays, lights ablaze in every window, the light of my life went out.

I stood beside his bed on that Christmas Eve after my five children had said their final farewells, holding his dear, dead hand and knowing that Handel's Messiah didn't apply to this situation. I could be a growing spiritual pilgrim with someone beside me pointing the way, cheering me on, telling me I could teach, get a doctorate and be a great wife and mother. Yes, I would even be a woman minister *(That was the bargain, God, if you would let him live)*. But I could not, (*Did you hear me, God?*) handle my own career, support the family, be a single parent to three grown children as well as Ron and Rob, both only nine . . . and wear Oscar's mantle of ministry.

As a child I had told my pastor, Rev. Koch, that I was afraid to die. He had laughed. "Don't worry," he chuckled. "You won't die for many years. And when you do, you will have dying grace. Why should God give it to you now and have you carry it around for years and years?" I looked at Oscar. The peace and joy, the dying grace of homecoming, was illuminating his face. That is the way to die, I thought. But as for me, where was my grace to go on living? I could not make myself let go of his hand and leave the room alone. His final words had been, "Make America see that it can happen anywhere and must happen everywhere." But at that moment I sensed the awful truth that I was alone. From now on, it was me and God, alone.

A chill ran through my weary soul. Finally it was real. Oscar was gone. I would have to turn around. The moment had come, though in my heart I knew I could not turn and go out alone.

Then the miracle happened. As I turned to do the impossible, I felt a presence so real, so genuine, so surprising, I almost shouted, "Why, I am not alone! I am not alone!"

Oscar had preached about the cloud by day and the pillar of fire by night. And now, in my darkest hour, I knew for the first time a presence that was lifting me to unknown heights, to heavenly places. "Blessed are the dead who die in the Lord" (Revelation 14:13). "Never will I leave you; never will I forsake you" (Hebrews 13:5). These were not cliches, but wings with which to mount up as an eagle, to run and not be weary, to walk and not faint (see Isaiah 40:31).

Was Oscar waving "goodbye" to me as he joined that great cloud of witnesses cheering me on from the grandstands? He must have been. No mortal can explain how I could be sadder than I had ever been before, yet happier than I had ever thought possible.

I went to the desk where those wonderful nurses stood tearfully bidding goodbye to a patient whose courage and faith had been his final ministry. I hugged them all. Could I explain what had just happened? "I just want you to know," I sobbed, "I am not alone. I'm going to make it just fine." For the first time in my life I really understood David's assurance, "Even though I walk through the valley of the shadow of death, I will fear no evil." Oscar's faith had become my faith, his God was my God, and I knew I could never be alone.

The memorial service for Oscar was held in the beautiful Lynn Memorial Campus Church of Central Methodist College. Organist Dorothy Solzman sat at the magnificent pipe organ. Friend, confidant, music mentor to our children since the days Oscar served in Hamburg, Iowa, she was playing Peer Gynt's Solveig's song for the Norwegian immigrant pastor who never returned to live in his native land. Now at his homecoming, Dorothy was playing the songs of Norway. I saw the heather on the hillsides, the goats at play, the fishing boats coming home laden with the day's reward. Yes, Oscar, your fishing vessel is coming in to port . . . heavy laden.

Robbie, our slow learner, who had come to us abused, deaf, almost blind and weighing only nine pounds at the age of one, reached over and tugged my arm. Pointing to the simple box adorned with a single rose, he whispered, "Don't be sad, Mama. That is just Papa's broken body." I should have been telling him that. All of his life Oscar had taught us that Christians know how to live. Now he was teaching us that Christians know how to die.

"The Lord bless, preserve and keep thee. The Lord make his face to shine upon thee. The Lord so fill thee with his Holy Spirit that in this world ye will serve him gladly, and in the world to come ye will have everlasting life." The great organ played the Hallelujah Chorus. The college president gave the benediction. Oscar had always concluded his morning benediction with "The worship is over, the service has begun." From somewhere it seemed I heard him declaring it for the final time.

We buried him under a majestic oak in the quiet cemetery next to the church he was to have served. The afternoon sun was casting great long shadows across the peaceful resting place. "You too shall be overshadowed by the Almighty" (see Psalm 91:1).

Country church funerals are social events. The women served chicken, beef and ham. Everyone brought desserts. They had already sent mountains of food to the house during the last days. I stood among them and wanted to thank them as I had done so many times for favors granted a parsonage family. But now I wanted to share more than just friendly thanks from the pastor's wife. I wanted to tell them how their kindness had ministered to my grieving heart, and how Oscar's courage, faith and vision had been his gift to me to share with them.

A dear saint in the church died the next day, and I had the funeral. I shared my faith and meant every word I said. But after I went home and tucked the boys in bed, the empty house echoed. I ached for the sound of a familiar Norwegian accent, for the hand that would never again reach out across the great expanse of emptiness in dark and lonely nights.

The next Sunday I climbed into the pulpit and preached on manna. Yesterday's manna spoils, tomorrow's cannot be garnered in advance. Only today's manna is suitable for today. Unfortunately, country churches don't have stained glass windows. While I was telling others to live for today I looked past the pews to that pioneer church cemetery, where snow flurries were whipping yesterday's wilted flowers from the fresh mound where I buried my lover and life. How I got through that sermon I am not certain. I only remember that before I stumbled from the pulpit, I announced my resignation. Dreams are wonderful, but reality is the stuff of which life is made.

A winter storm gathered while we were in church. Soon it unleashed its fury, whipping across the barren church yard. "Get in the car, boys." I said. "*Now.*" I was thankful for the storm. I would not have to say "Goodbye." Everyone would understand that what they were asking me to do was humanly impossible, call or no call.

The storm was wildly accelerating. Between the tears flooding my eyes and the angry walls of white blowing across my path, I hardly remember how we made it the forty miles back to campus. Twice we were stranded in the ditch. Snowplows, guardian angels in the Show Me State, pointed me home.

When we got home, I discovered I had forgotten to refill the oil barrel. The pipes were nearly frozen. Ron and Rob, who had been so brave, lost their courage. They needed solace. We built a fire in the fireplace. We took steaming hot baths. Nothing seemed to penetrate the cold. I was glad I would never have to make that trip again. I had kept my bargain with God; he had forgotten to keep his with me.

Grief has many stages. The courage and faith I had displayed during days friends and family were with me seemed gone . . . lost in the blinding blizzard. Taking their place in the cold, empty house of my heart were loneliness, anger, despair, desolation. *Surely, just this once, God, for all the times I have faithfully served, you could have let my bargain stick. What about faith healing, miracles, walking on water? Anything, Oh God, just anything!* I felt like a beggar at the king's table.

But I had not bargained with the unique people who make up a country congregation. Two hours after I had said my final wordless goodbye they stood half frozen, huddled and shivering at my front door. Having fought the sleet and the twenty-five below zero blizzard, there they stood, everyone who had accepted Christ during my bargaining days. The man who had lost his leg in a tractor accident was there. I had given him solace when I thought I had none. The family whose only daughter, a magna cum laude graduate, had committed suicide. I had helped them cope with death when I could barely cope myself. The young couple whose marriage had been falling apart had found faith and family while my family was disintegrating. They all stood at my door, braced against the December storm, comrades in my grief, asking me, "What do we do now?"

If country churches were constructed only of wood and bricks, nothing could kill them. But like everything that money can't buy, they are made of more fragile stuff . . . love and laughter, weeping and waiting, good dreams gone bad, bad dreams gone good, marryings and buryings, salt of the earth members and some less salty, and clergy of all strengths and weaknesses. They are built on strong foundations laid by pioneers who forged westward obeying Wesley's last command to Coke and Asbury as they sailed for a new land: "Offer Them Christ."

Nobody ever intends to kill a country church. Like good marriages gone bad, they die from neglect, apathy, lack of vision and well intentioned mismanagement. They die silently, one more every day across Methodism. Nobody hears the door bang shut on the faithful few. Sometimes they die yelling, sometimes weeping, sometimes almost without a whimper. It happens so gradually. First the youth and the children are gone, then nobody gets appointed at conference. Like patriarchal saints whose friends are all dead or have moved away, the door gently swings on its hinges for the last time. Someone goes over to dust when it seems fitting to bury an old pilgrim in the church of his childhood. Then everyone at the funeral sits there and remembers Christmas programs and the pieces they spoke, the old altar where so many found Christ and the men of God whose combined ministries consumed a lifetime.

Memorial Day finds old timers returning to judiciously weed overgrown ancestral graves, to shed a tear for what used to be and perhaps to mourn the demise of the rural church. Each year fewer graves are tended, and tombstones engraved "Beloved wife of" grow more difficult to read. Who remembers or cares whose beloved wife she was? Oh, yes, once it had meant everything. If ghosts of past pioneers could return, they might ask how, despite prairie fires, pestilence and plague, they could build what their affluent, educated grandchildren can only neglect amid prosperity and plenty.

But while everyone else said they were dead, Oscar always said country churches are made of something that never really dies. How can memory die, or faith, courage and perseverance? They merely slumber. All they need is a spark to rekindle them.

All this I knew by heart in my innermost being. But had I really believed it? Or had I been willing to yoke my life with Oscar's, to dream, to direct choirs, to teach children only because love believes all, hopes all, endures all? When ministers far less successful rose to positions of power, when the first question some pastors asked was "How big is your church?" had I stayed with him in the rural church because his dream was also mine?

The great moments of life often come quietly. The north wind beat fiercely against both my home and my unwilling heart. Stamping snow off sturdy cowboy boots, rubbing their hands over my anemic fire, even the burly farmers had tears in their eyes as they said, "If you leave, it will close again."

God had sent his unwitting angels on snow white wings to change the direction of my entire life. If it is true that we gain by giving, live by dying and that all any of us can hold in our cold dead hands is that which we have given away, then that day those saints in overalls made me eternally rich.

The men stoked the fire until the sparks flew. They needed a spark, and so did I. Their friendship was filling my empty heart and home.

The thought came to me that the combination of sparks make a dead fire glow. Maybe together we could warm the fires of faith. Oscar had always known that secret. Closed churches may revive because of the spark of one minister's fire, but the combined sparks of faith from each of God's saints makes the world want to warm itself at the hearth of the country church. Don't people say they want a "warm" church? That bone-chilling, bleak December Sunday afternoon we shared the spark that would make New Hope a church people would come from far and wide to see.

Some people make a decision and never look back. But most of us struggle and question. Jonah fled Nineveh. Moses protested that he was no public speaker. Like Peter I was learning that walking on water is a difficult skill to sustain.

The old arguments came back. If I were to take New Hope there would still be hundreds of other Methodist churches closing that year. I couldn't stem the tide. If I did expend all my spare energies, who could guarantee that others would carry on the dream when I left?

But I had my own reasons for letting the church die. Being the only woman on campus with a doctorate I had to work twice as hard to be considered half as good. I believed in equal pay for equal work and salary based on competency and credentials. But despite my years of experience and doctorate I was hired to teach twice as heavy a course load for $1,000 less than my male colleagues who did not have doctorates. My yearning for justice made me ask the president why.

"When you were hired, you were not head of your household."

"But now I am and always was. Oscar never taught here a day."

"Well, you signed a contract on that salary."

And if this discrimination existed in teaching, what about the ministry? I had been a good pastor's wife for twenty-seven years. I had played my part, presiding at the tea table or organ, whichever was needed, whenever it was needed. Just as willingly I had learned to give it up when decorum dictated. I had taught Sunday school—any time, any class without notice. I had learned to sing or be silent in the choir as the need arose, leading if that were the only way to have a choir, not leading if others wanted to serve. My psychology training had taught me how to calm the waters, how to stand as a buffer between fragile egos. This was the role for which I was prepared.

Anger is also a stage of grief. In moments of pain I almost dared to tell myself that God had failed me. I was now a single parent with three children in college and two high-risk adopted children at home to support. Working or being successful was no longer an option. My first obligation was to provide for my family. Dead churches take enormous love, work, time and money. Just as the acutely ill need intensive care, so do terminally ill churches. For Oscar, this fact had been a challenge, a calling he never doubted. One of the reasons we both worked for graduate degrees was so we could afford to spend our weekends opening closed churches. In an America gone mad with urbanization and reaping an aftermath of crime, drugs and family breakdown, the old country church was a back-to-the-basics answer. At a time when campuses were crowded with back-to-nature hippies seeking pleasure in drugs and a new morality, Oscar had been naive enough to believe that the back-to-nature country church was the genuine article.

Welfare, federal programs and counselors could never fulfill the intent of Matthew 25:35-36: "I was hungry and you gave me something to eat . . . I needed clothes and you clothed me, I was sick and you looked after me, I was in prison and you came to visit me." He believed that the country church at its finest is social worker and psychologist but far more importantly can even guarantee that "if anyone is in Christ, he is a new creation; the old has gone, the new has come!" (2 Corinthians 5:17).

New Hope United Methodist Church was not dying easily. Like Oscar, that tiny band of country folk had a rebuttal for my every protest.

"Your church is falling down," I said. "There is a hole in the ceiling where the coons have come in, and the wallpaper is falling off the walls." But they had done some arithmetic, and between them had pledged money to rebuild the church if I would stay. The fire crackled in my hearth while the winter storm raged. My heart knew a storm a thousand times greater as I faced the call of God to pick up Oscar's mantle *and do it alone.* No, not alone, but with the presence of the Holy Spirit and these sturdy people to guide me back on course.

3

Not a Secret Recipe

Winter spent its fury as it always does. The first crocuses poked their brave heads through the melting snows of March. Redbuds bloomed on campus. Trillium, white and fragile, heralded Easter. Wild cherry and crab apple scented the forest. Dogwoods, gentle reminders of the crucifixion, bloomed outside my bedroom window. Work, that gentle healer, had been a balm.

The boys had their paper routes. I had my teaching, writing . . . and now the church. On week days the boys delivered the Columbia *Tribune* on the bikes they had received that grim Christmas Eve when what they had really wanted could not be wrapped in gaudy paper and silver bows. When Sunday came and the papers bulged beyond bike capacity, I took them around in the car. This meant getting up at four and folding papers at the kitchen table. In the early morning I waited in the car while Ron and Rob carefully tucked the papers out of the snow and sleet at each front door. While the town slept, I prayed and rehearsed my sermons. Then it was home to hot chocolate before starting the forty-mile journey to church and the ceremony of breakfast at Colliers Junction to celebrate our survival of another week.

During those dark days of winter God sketched the plan for the new church clearly in my mind. Our Saturday visitation had paid off and the church was full. We needed more space.

March came in like a lion, forgetting it was the harbinger of spring. Snowdrifts buried every fence post. Pipes froze. Since I had no garage, the men at church installed an engine heater I could plug into the house current to help start my car in the wee Sunday hours.

Gentle April barged in like a bulldozer, breaking up country roads into pot holes and ruts and encrusting the car with mud for the children to wash off for a dollar each Monday. But a greater miracle than the changing seasons happened as the frozen ground began to thaw. I stood and watched workers eagerly dig the footings for a new church building at New Hope. I thought how they were building the very church Oscar had planned last spring. I looked beyond the men digging, past the old church, to a grave marked "Papa, Pastor, Beloved."

We had buried him there in the dead of winter. The surrounding fields, once lush with tall corn, had lain cold and barren, their useless, broken stalks grim reminders of a harvest long ended. My heart had felt as cold as the frozen corn fields. I stopped writing in my journal all winter. I read Shelley's immortal lines to my literature students: "If winter comes, can spring be far behind?" But what is springtime without love, without someone to share the robin's return, the lilacs in bloom? How could I bear springtime on campus with young lovers everywhere? I rationalized with Tennyson, "'Tis better to have loved and lost than never to have loved at all." I taught my psychology classes and counseled people and reminded myself that many people never experience, even for a moment, what God gave me for twenty-seven years.

Fortunately, our Heavenly Father indeed planned for spring to follow winter. Faith and love, those gentle counselors, had carried me through. Even though an hour always has sixty minutes, pain just seems less in a hurry than pleasure.

It was a turning point in my life. Spring was here. I had survived the winter. I began writing in my journal. Graduation was coming. Students were getting ready for new jobs, love and marriage. Optimism bloomed with the cherry trees and red buds along the Bonne Femme River and on the campus. I had sung through the long, dark night of winter just to keep my spirit alive. Now I sang for joy.

Springtime brought new life to Ron and Rob, too. The men of

the church, true to their promise to me when I accepted the church, became father to the fatherless. Each Saturday while I did my calling they taught Ron and Rob to drive tractors, feed hogs, mow hay and plant seed in faith. How happy I was for these good, happily married men who became role models for my sons.

That is when I affirmed again how God is marvelously the God of finances. I shall ever be grateful that Oscar had insisted I finish my education. My college salary was now able to help keep three daughters in school and provide for Rob and Ron. Oscar and I had always tried to give back to building funds any salary dying churches could afford. Oscar's financial legacy was the five thousand dollar insurance policy we had wisely struggled to buy over many lean years. Now, it was more money than I had ever had before. I needed to invest wisely.

When I led two students to the Lord, their father, who farmed one thousand acres next to the college, suggested that land was dirt cheap. He would put my five thousand dollars as a down payment on 140 acres next to the college, farm it for me, take his share and then reinvest the profits. Soon the farm was debt free and we were able not only to move to the country but to buy more land. This staunch Christian also became mentor for our boys and hired them during their high school years. It was this seed money which God multiplied to help build again and again dying churches.

All week long my hours were filled with students, faculty meetings, lectures, examinations, counseling and seminars. I loved my students—crying, rejoicing and suffering with them—but found myself also looking forward to Friday night when the academic world ended and I changed hats.

Slowly, silently, I sapped the stoic strength from the staunch rural families of New Hope. What laughter we shared as neighbors gathered, ice cream churns cranked and guitars accompanied favorite hymns. Wieners again tasted like those of my childhood as they sizzled over a bonfire of leaves the youth group had raked into a pile in the church yard.

Driving up and down the highways, I had planned the new church building. Having watched Oscar build one after another, I knew where to get lumber, how to get conference help and how to design it so that it would keep its country church charm, while meeting the needs of a congregation growing so rapidly that the old church could scarcely contain them all on Sunday. Pews were full. Young families were accepting Christ. While calling, I found family after family who had never been invited to a church. They were looking for a friendly country church where, away from the urban atmosphere, they could raise their children. Something stable and solid, a love of Mother Earth perhaps, is in all of us. People drove for miles to attend New Hope. They told their friends, and their friends also found Jesus Christ. Each person came with particular skills, answering a particular need.

New Hope is surrounded on three sides by sturdy Amish farmers, with their somber pie plate hats. Everyone said that selling land to the Amish had killed New Hope Church. As their clean, neat farms crowded closer and closer to the church, family after family moved away. But as we began building, the curious returned.

It was time to reach out beyond the surrounding Amish farms, and someone came up with the idea of a church bus. Even the most ridiculous idea must not be ignored for it may have been planted by God in that person's heart. The bus was exactly what was needed. Although we were surrounded by the Amish, we were the only church within eight miles. Dozens of homes nestled in the hills and hollows were untouched by any church. People were tempted to stay at home on Sunday, but if a bus stopped by, and if Sunday school offered treats and contests, and a country store exchanged tokens earned from attendance and bringing friends for prizes, they would come. We also used that bus for outings for the women and summer trips for the youth.

People often ask how every single closed church Oscar and I served revived. They want a "How to" booklet, as though they are asking a housewife who brought a carrot cake to the bazaar for her recipe. I believe it is a good question and an important one. I hope this book can suggest some usable ideas. But that is only the first part of the answer. The second part is to be willing to put forth the effort, energy, prayer and Holy Spirit power to persist until it happens. I watched those New Hope men in the springtime of my husband's death pour their sweat into building the very church Oscar had designed. I had always marveled at his ability to revitalize churches when he was alive, and now it was happening again. He was not here to suggest how to raise the funds or fill the pews. Even the plans he had sketched on a brown paper sack had been lost. But his vision was being set in concrete and fulfilled with two by fours as the proud congregation built a new and vital ministry out of the ashes of defeat.

Hear Your Calling

The first and most basic "how to" of church growth is to have a sure conviction of exactly what the purpose of the church is—what we are called to do.

Two shoe salesmen traveled to Africa to sell shoes. One returned shortly, saying, "You can't sell shoes in Africa—nobody wears them." The second never returned because he was too busy writing orders. Accompanying his bulging sales report was the jubilant note: "What a joy to be sent to a place where everybody needs shoes." If a church is closing, there must be all sorts of lost people around. And making disciples is the primary task of the church.

A pastor is just conducting a funeral if he only shepherds the faithful few who are left. A pastor is not called to confirm apathy but to equip for ministry. The faithful few are the cup of water that can be used to prime the dry pump. And when the stream of living water flows, everyone will drink and come alive.

I try to bring vivid objects into the sanctuary, such as a bird cage when I am preaching on "Wings to Fly," or twelve clothes baskets to illustrate the story of the loaves and fishes. One of my favorite props is an old hand pump. There's a story about a tourist who is lost in the great Mojave Desert. Parched and exhausted, he comes upon the kind of pump we had in our kitchen when I grew up. Tied to the pump handle is a whiskey bottle filled with water. He tries the pump. It doesn't work, and he is about to drink the water when he sees this note: "I know you're thirsty and are tempted to drink this water, but *don't.* Very carefully pour it into the pump. Then pump like crazy, and you will get water. If you drink it all up now you will die for sure. And be sure to fill the bottle up for the next guy."

The temptation, when you're about to pour the water into the well, is to say that the pump might not work, even if primed. Sixty percent of our churches never add a soul, year after year. We send pastors out until the priming water is gone and the pump dry, and then bemoan the parched corpses of churches found at too many country crossroads. Bishop Richard Wilke, in his book *And Are We*

Yet Alive? says we are an endangered species about which few are alarmed. Since 1965 we have lost half of our Sunday school enrollment and more than 3.7 million church members.

This is why the very first secret of reviving a closing church is to have a crystal clear vision of what the church and your call to it is all about. "Where *there* is no vision, the people perish" (Proverbs 29:18, KJV). Every pastor who is certain of a call must know that the business of the church is exactly as Christ defined it in his final words, "Go and make disciples of all nations" (Matthew 28:19). It is not preaching on Sunday. It is not building buildings. It is not going to meetings. A person is only a fisherman if he catches fish. If not, he may be a vacationer, a boat lover or a naturalist, but he is not a fisherman. Everyone, pastor and congregation alike, is called to be a fisher of men. If a pastor does not know how to win souls, he or she can learn. We have tried Evangelism Explosion, knucklepower door-to-door calling, leaving a gift package and a flyer about our church, Lay Witness Missions, child evangelism, open air Evangelism, one to one evangelism, revivals and a dozen other programs through the years. One is right for one church, one for another. A program that fails in one church may succeed in another. But no matter what approach is used, winning the lost and equipping them to win others is the sole task of the church.

Set Goals and Don't Stop Till You Reach Them

The second principle of church growth is to set goals and hold yourself responsible for them. I recently met a wonderful young man who played the lead in *The Music Man* for our church theatre group. He has a most unusual job selling Zephyrhills bottled water. My friend's company requires him to make 250 calls a day and sell Zephyrhills water coolers to fifty businesses or homes every day. If he doesn't he loses his job. I would hate to have his job, but he loves it and is enormously successful at it. He sets goals and he never stops until they are reached. We are selling the water of life.

Oscar had set goals the day we stood without benefit of key outside New Hope United Methodist Church. Looking through the windows, we claimed God's promises, saw it full to capacity and sketched the plan for new buildings. As we made a quick tour of the community, Oscar outlined where bus routes would go and noted which programs might be needed to make the doors swing open for all. He often said, "He who plans for defeat is never disappointed. But then neither is he who plans for success, because he can be certain he is in God's will, for God never fails."

Remember Whose Church It Is

Thirdly, make the people realize it is their church. Let them do it. Know how to work with people, how to discover their strengths. Delegate responsibility based on those strengths, and then reward and recognize success. The hundreds of notes laboriously written at the end of a busy day do pay off. Mention by name in the sermon, bulletin, newsletter or newspaper, every job well done. Oscar was great at enlisting both men and women, discovering their talents, and then delegating them to positions in which they were bound to excel.

It was good psychology and it paid off. A pastor can only meet goals if he or she lets others succeed in those goals that are God's will for them. Have them define their talents, then let them run with it. Trust them while being there and available.

This is not always easy. After years of church building, I have become pretty opinionated about some ideas that really work. For instance, since I have been assigned to churches in low income areas, I long for the churches we build to be the best looking and most inviting building in the community. I have often been aggressive in putting this vision before the people. However, I also believe it is impossible to build a church unless it is built in love and unity. When the majority opinion differs from mine, I write down twenty-five reasons why the other side might be right and give them the list. I have done this in churches. By giving people credit for their abilities, by delegating competent individuals to take responsibility and by giving them opportunities to make decisions, they often far exceed any ideas I might have had. And when the church building is completed, they can rightfully claim ownership for its beauty and its growth in spiritual unity.

Know How to Handle Money

Fourth, try very hard never to talk about money. Some district superintendents have suggested that this is wrong, that we should conduct an every-member canvass and preach on tithing. The cry everywhere is that churches do not pay their apportionments, have huge building debts or have to close because they have no money. However, in seventeen years of ministry I have never been appointed to anything but a closing church with a beggarly budget, and have left four strong churches which paid their apportionments in advance of January 1.

We have built buildings worth hundreds of thousands of dollars, but we have seldom driven a nail that was not paid for before it was hit with the hammer. We have received some grants but have refused long-term loans. No one is going to join a church that has seventy-nine members and owes eighty thousand dollars. If we assume that money not paid back is stolen, then by joining that church, a person would automatically owe one thousand dollars as his share. Such financial responsibility could well keep the lost out of our churches.

When Oscar and I became engaged, Rev. Nielsen (who had led me to Christ) called us in for a conference. I presumed he would talk about the birds and the bees. Setting us down before him, that venerable old saint said, "I have just one piece of advice for you two young people: Pay your bills. More ministers have failed, more churches have failed because they did not understand that money not paid is money stolen." I never forgot it.

To keep ourselves financially solvent, we refinished old furniture. I learned to tear apart old coats, turn the unworn side out and make beautiful new ones for our children. The Bible says, "Owe no man any thing, but to love one another" (Romans 13:8, KJV). I do not wonder that "owe" and "love" both appear in the same text. When a church or a pastor owes someone something he cannot or will not pay, it is impossible to maintain love. Plastic money, easy credit, the ability to indulge in debt whether on a national, personal or church level is destroying our country, our families, our churches.

How do you raise money to build debt-free churches? The answer is total commitment to Jesus Christ, to soul winning and to discipleship training. When we do this we set the stage for the final precept of church growth.

Create a Need

Fifth, create an obvious need. New Hope was empty when we came. It would have been futile to talk of building when the pews were vacant. The obvious need was to fill the pews we already had.

I have done church growth seminars in high steeple churches whose empty gymnasiums sit adjacent to slums where children do not have even a blade of grass for a playground. I have been asked to share in churches that have enormous empty education buildings surrounded by elementary, junior high and senior high schools. The obvious need is to match community needs with the facility you have. At New Hope, before we talked building, our obvious need was to create a program that needed a building.

You can't begin six new classes in a one room country church, especially when the lone heating stove bakes those closest to it and leaves everyone else frozen. Even if the room were large enough, the laughter from the children would be drowned out by the prayers of the seniors. It is difficult to build a youth program in the dead of winter, in a building twenty-four by sixty feet which has all the pews nailed down and no kitchen or rest rooms. And when it's thirty degrees below it's hard to ask seniors to march through a foot of snow to an outhouse. I learned never to drink coffee before going to New Hope; the necessary trek through the snow left my feet soggy and didn't enhance my sermon delivery.

At New Hope, the burgeoning congregation created a need, and it is a simple fact that when God's people see a need they respond without being begged or coerced or cajoled. None of us can turn away a hungry child from our door. Once a church sees that we are a spiritually hungry community, they give in total commitment for the sheer joy of giving. I saw it happen at New Hope and all the churches before and since. After the church was packed to capacity, the women held bake sales, children washed cars, men tilled the Lord's acre and the spirit of building and new beginnings was in the air.

Things That Aren't Taught in Books

But many things that all good pastors have learned can't be written down in a recipe book so that one, two, three, they make a church come alive. I remember our very first church. With fear and trembling, Oscar accepted a student pastorate at Oxford, Nebraska, in 1945. The salary was ninety dollars a month, plus ten dollars extra for cleaning the church. All week Oscar attended Hastings College many miles away. The dean had given him a corner of his basement for one dollar a week. With a hot plate and two dollars for stew meat, combined with vegetables from our garden, he managed to get a B.A. degree. He hitchhiked home on Friday night to save money.

The first Sunday we were ready to begin the service at eleven o'clock as announced. Not a soul was there. Being old world, Oscar was prompt. Being a visionary, he did not see the empty church. He visualized it full. He told me to start playing the piano, and he and I began singing.

By 11:20, twelve people were there. The itinerant preacher who had been helping before we were appointed had never started on time, so nobody ever came until 11:15. Oscar informed them that we had begun at eleven and would do so each Sunday.

That week we began calling door to door. By the next Sunday we had covered much of one side of town. It was just friendly visitation, introducing ourselves, telling about the church, carefully writing down each name as soon as we were away from the house, noting the number of children and young people. We recruited singers for a choir and teachers for Sunday school, and we jotted down anything interesting that could help build a program. We drank what seemed like gallons of coffee and iced tea and went home with six chickens, dozens of fresh brown eggs, a few roasts, one rabbit . . . and tired feet.

The next Sunday there were thirty-seven in church, and we started on time.

Nobody had told me that a minister's wife had to know how to play the piano, direct a choir, clean the church, make sick calls, pray over a dead dog, break up domestic quarrels and live alone five days a week while her new husband was away at college. Had I been born forty years later, I simply would have attended college with him and gone back weekends to help. But in 1945 the stereotypical minister's wife came with the package—two for the price of one.

The parsonage was a converted school house. Methodists think of conversion as a dramatic change, but the only change in this building seemed to be that partitions had been put up and a bathroom hung on as an afterthought. This convenience worked only in the summer; in the winter the water froze. The salary did not provide for heating oil. The farmers brought corn cobs which I burned in the stove in the kitchen, shutting off the rest of the house except on weekends when Oscar came home.

But our days were filled with joy. Having no children of our own yet, I began two afterschool clubs for children. I poured every ounce of my creative energy into those clubs, as though eternity depended on it. Soon, it seemed, every kid in town came thundering down the hill after school. We sang, had horrendous contests, gave marvelous prizes solicited from local merchants, put on plays, did magic tricks and learned Bible stories.

Every week some child accepted Christ. Soon more than two hundred children belonged to the club. They were invited to Sunday school, either at our church, or if they were leaning toward one of the two other churches in town, Roman Catholic and Presbyterian, their names were faithfully sent to our sister church. With no money for supplies, teachers cut pictures from Sears & Roebuck catalogs, old magazines or as a last resort, drew them free hand. These were pasted on flannel and faithfully marched across a felt covered board to illustrate Moses crossing the Red Sea or Jonah being swallowed by the whale. No child came to Sunday school whose family was not visited by us or a lay person.

Soon family nights, pot lucks, a circus complete with cotton candy and clowns who looked strangely like the pastor and his wife, harvest festivals and Easter egg hunts filled the calendar. No idea was too absurd to try. The old folks shook their heads. The young folks came, and soon we all melted into a family. But the heart of the ministry was Sunday morning when Oscar would preach his soul out and extend the invitation. That was the harvest of the week's toils. Many a family, bored or branded as failures, found a vital faith and a new love. Oscar believed the gospel should be life changing, lived in love and joy.

Our own love proved he was right. I lived for Friday nights when he would get home. Prayer meeting was at seven. He'd be there if the hitchhiking went well. I always had the lesson prepared in case he couldn't catch a ride. Train fare was out of the question. Later that night after everyone had left prayer meeting, our own private heaven began.

If there had been a funeral or wedding, we had fresh flowers on the table. If it were summer, corn flowers, iris or lilacs filled the air. And always, we had candle light and music. Regardless of what offerings of meat and produce had come to the parsonage, our finest wedding china and the Fostoria goblets that Dr. Stianson, who had gotten Oscar his scholarship to Northern Baptist Seminary, had given us for our wedding made it seem like a meal at the Hilton. This set the tone for our ministry. "Whatever you do for God, do it with class, with beauty, for God deserves your very best" was our philosophy.

I learned long ago that it doesn't matter how many clothes you have but how you match and wear them. We added touches of elegance to every church we built. Round tables seating six are much cozier than long benches. One new family would be carefully seated with two old timers and before the meal was over they felt like family. The women made white tablecloths and gathered candles and vases so families who could not afford restaurants could enjoy the romance of dining out even at a covered dish eatin' meetin'. How many years and churches our ministry spanned, each always seeming the loveliest and happiest.

4

Joy Comes in the Morning

Through the years, Oscar was active in work with the Family Court. If children needed a home, Oscar always brought them home. Two of these children, our precious Ron and Rob, we adopted. They were nine when Oscar died.

After his death, I got the boys a dog. They seemed to need something alive to love and care for to fill the void. For those first two difficult, lonely years after Oscar's death, Rex was their constant companion. He tagged along at their heels wherever they went and curled up at the foot of their bed at night. Psychologists say adopted and foster children always have a sense of emptiness that even loving adoptive parents can't fill. Rex came as close to filling that need as anything could.

I will never forget the day I heard a crash followed by an anguished cry from Ron. I rushed out to see him kneeling at the curb, clutching the mutilated body of Rex. A drunk had deliberately swerved his car to hit his target. "He died suffering, just like Daddy," sobbed Ron. "They meant to hit him, just like God meant to let Daddy suffer and die." Pain never wears kid gloves. It comes stealing back just when you think it has gone to sleep. Losing Rex meant nearly losing Ron. Ron didn't want another dog, just like he didn't want another father.

So I got Ron and Rob into scouting. Single mothers raising sons borrow father figures where they can. Bill Fisher, their scoutmaster, was a gentle soul acquainted with grief. Standing six foot three, he had broad shoulders, deep Irish eyes, a hearty laugh and a ready heart. He and the boys took to each other like ducks to water. He was a national scout executive turned nursing home administrator. After thirty happy years of marriage, Bill had lost his wife in a freak accident when a careless doctor gave her an inappropriate injection. Bill coped by returning to scouting.

He had always wanted boys of his own, and my boys filled his days and hours. They were soon inseparable. With the scout troop and without it, they explored the deep verdant forest which skirted the campus. Long years in scouting had taught Bill every bird call, and soon Ron and Rob could imitate the brown wren, the brilliant scarlet and black woodpecker and the mocking bird in the old walnut tree. One April Saturday after discovering the lair of a fox they came home and insisted I go with them. After that we became a foursome.

By the third spring after Oscar died, the church was built, and I was not crowding each day to keep from remembering. Sorrow is a hard taskmaster. I hadn't realized that for three years I had done almost nothing for myself. Neither had Bill, but this spring he had a thousand ideas. The circus was coming to town. We all went, ate the cotton candy and rode the Ferris wheel. I learned how good it was to laugh again.

We picked wild choke-cherries along the winding creek banks of the Missouri River. One Saturday when we had packed a picnic basket and were sitting along the riverbank, content with the day's catch of fish and love and laughter, Bill asked if he could go to church with us.

Bill was Irish Catholic and had attended parochial school. In his faith he had found the courage to overcome. His brilliant mind was cloaked in a childlike faith that never questioned God and accepted life or death as a gift. We talked often of our faith. While I often felt the cross heavy, he felt it an honor to be entrusted with it. He knew I was a clergywoman, but he had never heard me preach. Would he think differently of me in this new light? I treasured our friendship and did not want to change anything. Would our relationship be the same once he realized what my call meant in time and service? His church did not ordain women, yet he accepted my calling without question.

The four of us went to New Hope the next Sunday. Bill was strangely moved by that service. We spent that afternoon on the back roads of the Amish community. We looked for their delicious homemade fudge but learned they didn't sell it on Sunday. We did find their meeting house surrounded by black shiny buggies and plainly dressed boys and girls playing hopscotch. I admired their simplicity, their faith and their fairness in dealing with others. People are called in so many different ways.

Bill asked me about my call. Was it different from the call he had felt to work with scouts or the retarded and elderly people at his nursing home? He told how he had once felt called to be a priest. But the war had come, and he had fought through the grim days of North Africa until the invasion of Italy, seeing too much death, accumulating too many memories. Afterward, scouting had seemed to be a better way to do penance for having had to kill and maim. Perhaps in scouting he could be the father confessor to hundreds of boys before they had to go to war. And so this had been his ministry. Yes, he understood my call. I knew I had met someone with the perception to understand why I had to carry on Oscar's unfinished vision, and why it had finally become my own.

The next week when the boys returned from an awards banquet wearing their scout uniforms they told me the three of them had a surprise for me. Bill handed me a tiny box. All three saluted and said, "A scout is honest, loyal, true, faithful . . . and we three scouts would like you to marry Bill." They had all three picked out a simple wedding set, designed in the pattern of a rose. I knew for certain God was calling me to love again.

Dr. Randolph Nugent, head of the Methodist Board of Global Ministries, invited me to New York to look into an available position as head of the Division of Higher Education. He had to hire a women clergy who had a doctorate in Education and college teaching experience, and I fit the bill. The BOGM flew me to New York, then to Chicago to meet the Board.

I was eligible for tenure at the college that spring. The rules said professors must first teach four years in the college—two years if they had two years previous college teaching experience. I had the previous college teaching experience but was told to wait four years anyway. The college president called me into his office.

"I know the offer you have before you. Are you going to take it?" he asked. How had he heard?

"I don't know. I don't have tenure here. I have excellent evaluations, but my salary is below the men's, even though I am a single head of household. What security do I have here?"

I was astounded at his reply. I knew his job at the college was shaky; we changed presidents often during those troublesome days when university presidents were locked out of offices. I liked him, but many professors opposed any authority. With a straight face he said, "Turn it down, recommend me, and you'll have tenure in your mailbox today."

I talked the situation over with Bishop Robert Goodrich. He examined my Bachelor of Religious Education transcript from Northwestern and Northern Baptist Seminaries. I had studied Greek, homiletics, hermeneutics, doctrine, church history, psychology, exegesis, senior preaching, pastoral ethics—140 hours in all, including many hours of Bible. "You qualify for ordination and conference membership," he said. "We need you. I'll see you get it." I passed the Board of Ordained Ministries. I talked to my ex-bishop, Bishop Frank. He advised that the BOGM job was a token position, and whoever got it would be fired in a year. (He was right.) I turned it down, even sending back my plane fare. I recommended the president for the job. Finally, I had secured both tenure and ordination.

Bill and my children were with me when the bishop asked the holy questions: "Have you faith in Christ? Are you going on to perfection? Do you expect to be made perfect in love in this life? Are you earnestly striving after it? Are you resolved to devote yourself wholly to God and his work? Do you know the General Rules of our Church? Will you keep them? Have you studied the doctrines of the United Methodist Church? After full examination, do you believe that our doctrines are in harmony with the Holy Scriptures? Will you preach and maintain them? Have you studied our form of church discipline and polity? Will you support and maintain them? Will you diligently instruct the children in every place? Will you visit from house to house? Will you recommend fasting and abstinence, both by precept and example? Are you determined to employ all your time in the work of God? Are you in debt so as to embarrass you in your work? . . . "

Bishop Goodrich, the clergy, Bill and my family laid hands on my head as I knelt, tearstained, at the altar of the college church. I was called, ordained, set aside for ministry and assured I was an associate member of the Missouri East Conference. I arose feeling even closer to God than when I had said goodbye to Oscar. Just as I had been touched by God at age twelve when I gave my life to Christ, I now felt that same touch giving me a new and final direction.

It had been three years since I had promised New Hope I would serve them. I had kept my promise. Although a dying church can hardly refuse a woman pastor, the idea of a Catholic clergy spouse seemed too much for me. Bill said he would become a Methodist, but I said, "No. I am not marrying you to change you. If I didn't love you the way you are, I wouldn't marry you. I will go to mass with you on Saturday nights, and you can go to my church on Sunday if you wish." I knew for certain he was a Christian.

Fortunately, our mission program had taught the people at New Hope about the inclusive church, which is not bound by color, wealth, rank or denomination. Catholics, Amish and Baptists had all cheered us on as we built.

"What in the world is wrong with a Methodist woman minister having a Catholic husband?" they reasoned in unison. They asked us to postpone the wedding a month so they could put the finishing touches on the sanctuary and install air conditioning. We did and it seemed the entire countryside turned out to celebrate with us—the Amish, the Catholics, the Baptists and, of course, the Methodists.

To honor the Irishman, we had green candles, wore green dresses and sang "My Wild Irish Rose." It was the first wedding in the completed church. I looked around at those who had shared my pain, and I theirs. These honest, earthy country people had guided me through the night of sorrow. I felt confirmed in my call to spend the rest of my life opening country churches.

The president emeritus of Central Methodist College, Dr. Woodword, married us. He read, "Weeping may remain for a night, but rejoicing comes in the morning" (Psalm 30:5). The young people decorated our car, tied tin cans on it and threw rice. The last thing I heard as we headed for our Jamaican honeymoon was the entire congregation singing "Praise God from Whom all Blessings Flow."

Our days were filled with love and laughter. As we spent cold winter nights around the fire, just sitting, reading and talking, I knew that Job was right. I had always wondered how he could have lost his wife and children and possessions, got them back again and believed that the end was better than the beginning. Now I knew it was because he had matured. He had walked with God through the valley of lamentation and come to the mountaintop appreciating as never before the good gifts God sends.

Each September, like an old circus horse who longs for the sawdust ring, I smelled chalk and blackboards. I loved the campus, the fellow teachers and students of Central Methodist College. Every season had its charm. Autumn brought brand new freshmen, apprehensive parents in tow, to register and settle into the dormitories. On crisp winter mornings hoarfrost would silhouette every barren twig making Central a winter wonderland.

But all that was but a prelude to spring, when the entire campus exploded with tulips, jonquils and redbuds, like a bridal bouquet set amidst the dazzling white of cherry blossoms.

Never had I felt so creative. My classroom was filled with a hundred ideas for budding teachers to make and take into their new world. My office was filled with students from my psychology and education classes coming to share, to unburden, to find direction. What a joy to be on a Methodist campus where each one could be confronted with God's plan for his or her life.

Bill and I bought a new nursing home to provide a home for people with mental retardation who were by legislation being placed back in the mainstream of society. Bill instigated the building of a sheltered workshop for mentally retarded persons in our county. No longer would they sit aimlessly rocking back and forth, robbed of their dignity. Now they would have a chance to feel pride in earning some money and take their place in society. Not only was Bill a beautiful part of my growing ministry at New Hope, but I became a part of his ministry, too.

Oscar had been gone nearly eight years. Each spring I planted geraniums, petunias and marigolds on his grave and in profusion around the church. What had once been almost impossibly painful was now comforting and reassuring.

"Therefore, since we are surrounded by such a great cloud of witnesses, let us throw off everything that hinders and the sin that so easily entangles, and let us run with perseverance the race marked out for us. Let us fix our eyes on Jesus, the author and perfecter of our faith" (Hebrews 12:1-2). Is this "great cloud of witnesses" the sainted dead who have retired to the grandstands while we play the game of life? If so, maybe I had been given Oscar's number. I had felt his spirit with me so many times, almost as though he were looking over my shoulder.

"How should the altar be designed?"

"I'd make it like this."

"Paneling or Sheetrock here?"

"Remember what we did back in Nebraska?"

"Right, I had forgotten how great that looked."

Often I would stand alone in the quiet church and be surprised to hear a chuckle .... almost surprised to realize that it was my own.

"What shall I preach about today?" Countless times I had said "Thanks for the idea," not knowing if the gratitude was directed at the Almighty or Oscar. As time passed it became increasingly clear that he was not in that quiet rural churchyard. It was not his grave that comforted me, but his spirit alive in me.

There are two routes to conference membership and ordination: seminary and the five year course of study. Since I already had five degrees when I entered the ministry at age fifty, I opted for the course of study. During the summers I attended Perkins Seminary in Dallas and St. Paul's in Kansas City. When the Board of Ministry told me my records had all been lost, and I would have to begin the process of conference membership all over, I showed them my deacon's orders. (For eighteen years the United Methodist Church was going to be bewildered at how I could be a deacon, have had the hands of the bishop laid upon me, and not be an associate member of the conference.) But one does not argue with the Board of Ministry when the call of God is upon one's life, so I began the process all over again . . . examinations and psychological testing.

By 1978 it was all done, and I stood before the Board again, my credentials in hand. I also took along my deacon's orders. That is when I first heard about Clinical Pastoral Education. I did not qualify for conference membership until I had completed an internship in CPE. If I would perform a six month internship in a hospital, I would complete my work. I went to the University of Missouri, where my doctorate had been granted, and secured a scholarship for training in Clinical Pastoral Education, but I was too busy at the time to fit it in. Maybe I would get a sabbatical next year, I thought. I asked to work on the critical care floor. I wanted to learn to face death so that I would never flee from it again.

It had been a long pilgrimage since that first sermon when I had tried to escape after the service. It was six years since I had been ordained and assumed I was an associate member of the conference. I had completed the training I had been told I needed. Although I had seen other women put off time and again, I was still not willing to say "discrimination." If I were to serve the United Methodist Church, I must honestly feel a sense of loyalty and devotion to it. Whatever tests, whatever hurdles —these were but to strengthen my call.

That stance was sorely tested, however, when I began to hear rumors that New Hope, which seven years before was almost closed by the bishop, was now one of the choicest rural appointments in the conference. Since I did not have conference membership, I was not eligible for appointment to a church of its size. Bill, always loyal, laughingly advised me to apply for priest in his church. After a discouraging session with the Board of Ministry, how refreshing it was to come home and be held close while he told me, "Cheer up. If you were a clergyMAN, I'd never have fallen in love with you."

5

The Cruelest Month

Christmas came. Ron and Rob were sixteen now. We cut two trees, a huge one for the college, another for the house. Danes know how to celebrate Christmas! We followed the centuries old traditions . . . rice for the Nissa, roast pork, aeblekage, the tree decked with cornucopias filled with pfeffenusse, woven paper baskets filled with peppermints and paper angels. It was eight years since I had stood by Oscar's bedside, said goodbye and had the marvelous gift of God's presence assuring me I would not be alone. God had been more than faithful. I had counted on his presence alone to sustain me in the ministry. He had given me that indeed, but he had further blessed me by giving me Bill to share the thrill of building up New Hope, board by board, heart by heart, soul by soul.

After our Christmas pageant at New Hope, everyone in Sunday school received gifts. Then sleighbells jingled on the roof and a raucous, strangely familiar Santa Claus distributed candy and oranges to good boys and girls of all sizes. For the pastor's family there were packages of the finest steaks from a recent butchering, mouth-watering black walnut fudge and offerings of cookies and Christmas breads as each person said "I love you." We had to open all the gifts then and there. A thousand volumes couldn't describe the warmth and devotion of this rural tradition or the unspoken value of the hugs that stamped "Paid In Full" on any sacrifice made by the misty-eyed recipient. I stood there a millionaire in assets of chicken, roasts, candles, blouses, crazy ties for Bill, a treasured Bible from the congregation, toys and clothes for the children, gifts so carefully chosen that I wept my way through the mound of beribboned love.

I knew then why the evangelism of love works. Mose, a faithful worker at Bill's nursing home, once told me, "You can't no more give somebody something you ain't got than you can come back from some place you ain't been." He was right.

One new member, full of Christmas love, said to me that night, "I hope our church never grows so big that we lose this."

"It has to grow," I replied. "Think what would have happened if we had decided the church was just the right size before you came. But it doesn't ever have to lose this. 'He that loves knows God, because God is love'" (see 1 John 4:7).

But as much as I loved Christmas at the church, I lived for our family celebration of Christmas at home. It was a special time when exams were over, students had gone home, and for one sparkling week the church folks would be busy with their families and we with ours. In 1978, that sixth year of our marriage, my eighth year at New Hope, the world was never better. The fragrance of the crisp brown turkey wafted from the kitchen, and Bill and I sat alone thanking God.

Then, without warning Bill began to hemorrhage. I raced to the phone, called the ambulance and notified the VA hospital that he was enroute. I shut my ears, my heart, my mind. I couldn't believe I heard the doctor say "leukemia," "transfusions," "fatal," "make plans."

The next day he was better and optimistic. He came home and we reveled in those after Christmas, do nothing days. I denied that anything had happened and put it out of my mind. We would beat this, us two and our call, with God on our side.

We attended a healing service. Bill prayed for healing, and came home assured that he was healed. There is no doubt he was healed in spirit. His life literally glowed with Christ. He finished his community campaign for the sheltered workshop. We remodeled the nursing home, making it more beautiful and homelike. Never before had it been so filled with music, laughter and love and the Spirit of Christ. Never before had we felt so perfectly in God's will, so close to the Great Physician, until the February day when a mere transfusion was not enough.

The weeks that followed seemed like a recurring nightmare. Surely I wasn't hearing the same message again. I begged to hear them say "remission" or "time." I clung to only the upbeat part of the doctor's report. Maybe transfusions, or new medication . . . I examined my own life. I prayed the long nights through. Was there anything God wanted of me? Was there any bitterness or unforgiven sin? The love and support of our New Hope family helped sustain me.

One Sunday, the district superintendent came to preach. It was time for a pastor who was a conference member to be appointed to New Hope.

I pleaded with the Board of Ministry. "I have been ordained. I have completed the five year course of study."

"You need six months of Clinical Pastoral Education," was the reply. "You need to go through the entire process again. Maybe then you will pass."

It was far too painful to say goodbye to New Hope. I asked the district superintendent to do the honors for me. They wanted to give me a farewell party, but my pain was too acute. I was awaiting another goodbye.

And then it was April. On sunny days, after a transfusion, Bill would be healthy and laughing, defying every prediction of the doctors. Then, as we lay close to each other in the middle of the night, he would begin bleeding internally. We would race to the hospital, fearful as two fawns with the hunter in pursuit.

I had been able to understand death in the dead of winter, when the leaves are buried deep beneath the snow, when every tree limb shivers cold and naked against a sullen winter sky. But death in the springtime, when crocuses are blooming and jonquil and lilac scent the air, bursting with new life, is ironic. It is a rebuff. It is unbelievable. *That* is what happened.

Spring never came for me that year. The winter winds of anguish blew frantically against my aching heart as I signed the permission to give his body for research, as he had requested.

Ron went to see Bill the night he died. Sobbing in pain, he fled from the hospital. He said he was running away from home, from a God who could do this to all of us. Rob reacted differently. He cried and cried and cried. I held him close and sobbed with him. I cried out for Ron as we searched the city for him.

By morning the police had picked him up as an accomplice with another boy who had stolen five dollars. He was in jail, and later would stand in court and plead guilty to theft.

The memorial service for Bill was held in the beautiful chapel on Central Methodist Campus. All the college family was there, as well as the ministers of the conference and town. Most comforting of all was the family of the New Hope United Methodist Church.

The only one who wasn't there was Ron. I had asked to have him released but was told he could only come in handcuffs and foot-shackles with a paid guard at his side. I wonder what healing that service might have been to him. I will never know.

The dark night of my soul became wrapped in the dreadful despair of Ron's being in prison. On my first visit, I drove to the high barbed wire fence, tried to go in but sat sobbing in the cold, dismal rain, unable to initiate myself into that vast fraternity of prison mothers. In sorrow I drove all the way home. The next day, courage came. But no matter how many times I visited Ron, I never left without my heart being torn in a million shreds for every inmate.

For five years I visited the prison weekly and learned more about the penal system than I ever cared to know. I went as a counselor and therapist working with Dr. McKinney, head of the University of Missouri Psychology Department, who had been a member of my doctoral committee. We became close friends, comrades in ministry. I came to understand why Jesus lumped those in prison with those who were naked and hungry. My heart broke for so many who in one fatal moment had sealed their fate for a lifetime.

I applied for Clinical Pastoral Education at the University of Missouri Medical Center, asking for the terminal care floor. I had a handle on death now . . . I felt I must find a positive reason for it by helping others.

There was a month left until the end of school. The president, bless his heart, called me to his office one day and suggested that I was eligible for a year of sabbatical leave. I said I would like to take it, although I had no idea what I would do with it, aside from completing my CPE.

First I had to sell the nursing home. This was not easy, not because nobody wanted it, but because it was not a hardware store. The mentally retarded people living there had become my family. They wept at Bill's death, mourning for the loss of the parent he had been to them. The day of the funeral, a friend had asked what she could do. I said, "Go home and clean out Bill's closet. Take everything to the men at the nursing home."

It was painful but helpful to me to see our beloved Henry wearing the jacket Bill wore when we were married. Henry could only say, "See, Bill gives me." If we didn't watch him, he would have worn it to bed. He never wanted to take it off. Who was I to tell him he was wrong? I knew exactly how he felt.

To be single again in a married world was not a new experience for me. But the first time I had been encircled by the church. A minister always has a family when he or she has a church. A minister is a standing member of every organization in the church. Whether it's youth or seniors, singles or married folks, a minister is not a fifth wheel. But this time I was not a part of any church. I began looking for one. I felt out of place.

For the first time I realized that churches are designed for happily married couples. There are usually some older widows, a single parent or two and a few divorced persons trying to fit in, but often there are no real programs for them. I began to wonder what happens to the half of America that lives single in a world of couples.

I decided that, with an entire year to do whatever I wanted, I would try to find out. Rob, after years of special programs with Vocational Rehabilitation, was ready for independent living. He had been accepted at Teen Challenge, where the good leadership of the director, Herb Meppelink was a positive influence.

I learned of a visiting scholar program at Harvard University. After prayer, I was certain this was where I wanted to go. I sent my credentials, and the return mail brought my acceptance. I would begin my studies at Harvard in the spring semester of 1980.

There was a month left in the school year, and then I had to finish my Clinical Pastoral Education and sell the nursing home. I completed the remodeling of the nursing home and planted flowers everywhere. I wanted to leave the finest, most beautiful memory of Bill possible for each resident.

I looked forward to Harvard. As a visiting scholar, I could cross reference to any school on the campus. I would take courses in reading, testing and psychology and cross reference to the Divinity School as I followed my hunch about the church's ministry to singles. I would go to Cambridge the next January. Was the ministry behind me? Probably, I thought, but I would do the CPE anyway to keep the doors open. I would have paid my dues. With my tenure intact, I would be back teaching at the college after my sabbatical year.

When God closes a door he does it gently. Had I known the day I turned in my grades at the college that I would never again teach there, I don't believe I could have endured the sadness. The years at Central Methodist College had been filled with meaning. I had taught in the Psychology, Counseling and Education Departments, all disciplines with the potential for changing students' lives. But the teaching had also changed me. I'd had more opportunities for growth and achievement than I'd ever dreamed possible.

I turned in my grades, marched in the graduation ceremony with my cap and gown and hood and sat there looking at those fresh young faces, eager to go out and conquer the world.

There was a new fad on college campuses across America that year. At graduation the class would throw a pie in the face of their favorite teacher. A student had warned me that I had been chosen for this dubious honor. Although it was a backhanded way of saying, "You are one of us," I didn't feel at all in the mood, and slipped quietly out the side door. I had already said too many goodbyes this year.

6

Loaves and Fishes

When Oscar died, farmland had been at its lowest price in years. I had wisely invested his five thousand dollar insurance policy in 140 beautiful, rolling acres of farmland, resplendent with hundreds of sturdy oaks, hickory, ash, wild cherry, redbud and the giant pine trees which became the fifteen-foot Christmas trees for the college dances and the high-ceilinged church sanctuary, as well as our old-fashioned Danish Christmas tree at home. On spring mornings at the farm, wild daises, violets and blue bonnets scattered their vibrant colors across the fields and along the five ponds. There Bill and I had caught many a fine line of catfish. The land had been a corner of heaven, a retreat for spirit and body, a place for raising the boys. No country pastor can serve well until he understands what Tara meant to Scarlet O'Hara. Each evening as I'd turn down the lombardy poplar-lined ribbon of farm road, my heart was at home. For this Scandinavian warrior, it was Valhalla.

Bill always said I could go from high heels to sneakers faster than anyone he knew. In the daytime I was professor and mentor, and Bill was a nursing home administrator, president of the Rotary and a member of the Chamber of Commerce and City Commission.

But on the farm we were free to wear jeans and an old T-shirt while branding cattle and birthing piglets.

A gentle rain was falling on the rolling hills as I stepped out on that lovely old farmhouse porch. I had to think, to be alone, to sort things out. Had I shed Oscar's mantle? Could I escape the call of God, the deep conviction that I was still ordained in the Methodist church and that my call was forever? In the solitude of the rain, I sang my heart out: "When he shall come with trumpet sound, O may I then in him be found! Dressed in his righteousness alone, faultless to stand before the throne!"

Then God bowed the sky with a dazzling rainbow from horizon to horizon. Like a smile from heaven, I seemed to hear the answer, and I sang it back: "My hope is built on nothing less than Jesus' blood and righteousness. I dare not trust the sweetest frame, but wholly lean on Jesus' name."

"In the last days, God says, 'I will pour out my Spirit on all people. Your sons and *daughters* will prophesy, your young men will see visions, your old men will dream dreams. Even on my servants, both men and women, I will pour out my Spirit'" (Acts 2:17-18, Joel 2:28-29, italics mine). I had an uncanny feeling that I was about to continue as one of those Methodist visionaries who planted churches a day's journey apart in every village. At revivals and camp meetings, circuit riding preachers daring wind and rain and hail, preached Jesus Christ loud and clear. Souls were saved and Methodism swept like wildfire across America.

Somewhere a million miles away I heard the phone ringing. Let it ring. In my reverie, Bishop Goodrich was laying his hands upon my head again and asking the sacred questions.

"Have you faith in Christ? Are you resolved to devote yourself wholly to God and his work? Will you preach and maintain the Holy Scriptures? Will you observe the following directions? Be diligent. Never be unemployed. Never be triflingly employed. Do not mend our rules, but keep them, not for wrath, but for conscience sake."

"*Yes, Yes, Yes*!"

The phone kept ringing. I knew who was calling. As always, it was God. The conference might not acknowledge it, but I could never deny it. That was all that mattered. I was a part of that great army of Wesley's pioneers.

A call is not contingent on conference membership or guaranteed appointment. Had the bishop not asked, "Are you convinced that you should enter the ministry? Are you willing to make any sacrifices involved? Are you willing to make a complete dedication of yourself to the highest ideals of Christian ministry? Will you keep before you as the one great objective of your life the advancement of the kingdom of God?" To all this I had said a resounding *yes*! Could I ever be uncalled? The answer was *no*!

I picked up the phone. It was the district superintendent. The nearby Red Rock and Hallsville churches were closing. Would I be interested in preaching there this summer until I left for the Harvard? I didn't hesitate.

"Yes, but I want every day to count toward the four years you are now requiring for conference membership. I want to do my CPE two mornings a week this semester. I want full minimum salary so each day I serve can be counted full time." I wanted justice. The United Methodist *Discipline* says, "Itinerancy is that system by which ordained ministers are guaranteed appointment." For six years I had been ordained but denied every secular and sacred right of ordination.

The Monday night after graduation found me with my guitar tucked under my arm meeting with the last four faithful people at Red Rock Methodist Church in their crumbling, hundred-year-old structure. But I don't recall seeing that church old or empty or decaying. As I entered the church, I saw it full . . . as it would soon be. I saw it rebuilt, enlarged, growing and glowing.

Little did I know that the leader of the Missouri Outlaw dance band, the best lead guitarist in Missouri, was among the four faithful. I never took my guitar out of the case, but it had done its work. It had caught his attention, and by the end of the evening we had scheduled a Saturday outing on my farm that included a hayride for the children, swimming in the Fayette pool, a treasure hunt and a ball game in the pasture. The day finished with a country gospel sing that rocked Howard County. Afterwards, I shared the marvelous love of Jesus and told what he had done for me and what I knew he could do for them.

When everyone had gone home, I could not sleep. The bed was too empty, the house too quiet. A mellow June moon was shining through my window. I dressed, got in my car and drove to

Hallsville and Red Rock. I quietly slipped off my shoes and walked around each church, claiming them for God and dedicating myself and that spot as holy ground.

It was midnight when I headed back across the hills. I turned the car north and drove by New Hope on the way home. The full moon was shining down on the marigolds on Oscar's grave, surrounded by so many saints I had planted until the resurrection day. Maybe Harvard was ahead, maybe it wasn't, but for this summer I knew my call.

It was almost morning when I returned from my pilgrimage. Trillium dotted the roadsides and redbuds embellished the pastureland. A rooster crowed his welcome while a newborn calf found his equilibrium.

Then and there I knew how we would get a new roof on the Red Rock Church. We would have an "all church" auction. Like the Israelites of old, I would lead the way with the best of my herd.

The Columbia *Tribune* got word of the auction. The television cameras were there, along with the entire community of Hallsville and Red Rock. Everyone had brought something to sell . . . old cars, trash and treasures, and the lady preacher's coal-black, purebred Angus calf. Folks bought the calf and gave it back to be auctioned and sold again. It sold six times. I was the final bidder. I named it Red Rock, and returned it to the lush pasture where it had been born.

The next morning both churches were fairly full. In a unique way, the church had awakened the community and gotten its attention. The TV cameras returned the next month when forty men began building a new roof. The women brought bulging picnic baskets. I was sent up to inspect the roof once, but for the most part, I simply sat at the picnic table talking to new people. Some of them ended up dedicating themselves to Jesus Christ as Lord and Savior and to Red Rock Church.

Some who missed the auction wanted to give money. When we finished the roof we had enough money left to add a new front to the church, and when that was finished the men drew plans for a whole new addition.

My introduction to the Hallsville church was quite different, but no less miraculous.

Every country church has a wonderful junk and treasure room, usually stuck under a stairwell. In such a dank, dusty, chilly closet

God and I won our first victory at Hallsville. I was rummaging for anything salvageable to recycle for Sunday school material when I discovered Mary and Joseph and the creche, but no Baby Jesus. I heard a shuffle on the staircase and looked up to discover that a veteran saint had come by to see what that fool lady preacher was doing on her knees in the bowels of the furnace closet.

Learning of my quest she retorted, "You won't find Jesus here. Some kid swiped him off the manger scene years ago. That's when we stopped putting it up. It's time to close the church when folks don't care no more than to swipe Jesus."

Together we sat down on the old packing boxes and I preached my first sermon in Hallsville. I explained to her that stealing Jesus wasn't half as bad as what they had really done to him that Christmas two thousand years ago. Didn't they shut the door on him at the inn and wasn't his delivery room a lowly manager? And, didn't that beautiful, chubby manger baby grow up to be spit upon? Scourged and guiltless, wasn't he nailed to an old rugged tree for *our* sins?

That gave my friend an idea. Next Christmas, why not put out the creche without the Baby Jesus and let our church supply Jesus to everyone who needed him?

I didn't stumble for sermon material the next Sunday. To the tiny few gathered I suggested that we had exactly what this town needed. We had Jesus. He was never meant to be hoarded for one's self. If everyone would bring a new Baby Jesus between now and Christmas we would advertise that the Baby Jesus at Hallsville Methodist Church was for the taking: "If you don't have a doll for your little child, in the name of Jesus, come take the one in our manger."

The dolls began arriving. One grandmother, far from her own children, dressed up a cherished doll from bygone years. A teenager brought one she had outgrown. Suddenly, dolls were all we talked about. In fact, by the time the Columbia *Tribune* carried the story and Christmas was in the air, dolls were piled high in the church. Each doll that was taken anonymously was replaced with one even more cherished.

I shall never forget the father of eight, unemployed until a week before Christmas, who knelt in the snow, making the sign of the cross and hugging close to his heart the Elkin's Raggedy Ann.

Maybe it didn't look like the Baby Jesus—but maybe it did. Tears filled my eyes.

"Don't go away," I called and ran out to him with my arms full of Baby Jesuses. "Here, take these," I proffered, my arms filled with a doll for each of his cherubs.

"Oh, no, I couldn't," he ventured. "It would be too much."

"Nonsense," I whispered. "Take Jesus. There's enough of him for everyone."

"And there still is," I said to myself as he drove into the December whiteness.

We had a glorious Christmas at Hallsville and Red Rock. Both churches were now filled to bursting. I was due at Harvard in a week. The people said they would help with the calling while I was at Harvard. I talked to the district superintendent who said the visiting scholar program was a legitimate study leave after eight years in the ministry. It was agreed I would study at Harvard three days a week and fly home to serve the churches the other four.

Harvard was all I expected. Oscar and I had lived in Harvard Square thirty years earlier when he was at Boston University. I had loved the cobblestone streets, the Charles River, walks down to the Square, Longfellow's home, the yard and historic dorms where presidents from Roosevelt to Kennedy had studied.

I delved into a study of the church's ministry to divorced persons. I loved research—its precision, its honest attempt to find statistical answers. I did an analysis of covariance, taking a random sample of divorced people. I asked them what significant ministry the church had offered to them at the time of their divorce, and what ministry the church had provided their children. I followed those who had been faithful in the church at the time of their divorce to find out if they remained faithful. I visited every church in the greater Boston area to learn what viable programs existed for divorced people. I began a singles group in the churches back home to see if I could prove my conclusion.

The time passed quickly. Every moment was filled. I had little time to think of grief.

But by the end of the seventh week I suddenly had much more to think about. One Saturday morning when I was home from Harvard for the weekend, a police officer knocked on my door at four a. m. asking me if I knew where Ron was. Ron had been in a holding tank with fourteen other inmates, had been threatened with sexual abuse and had escaped during a yard break. I was crushed. I cried to God during long sleepless nights praying for Ron's safety. When I went back to Harvard, I arranged my research so I could complete it at home and returned to Missouri to be near Ron should he return.

Ron was caught and, unable to see himself as worthy, deliberately denied himself any chance of leniency. I hired the best possible lawyer to no avail. Ron pled guilty, waived all rights, and was sentenced as an adult (he had just turned seventeen when Bill died) to five years in prison for being an accomplice to a boy who went free though he had stolen the five dollars. This Gethsemane led me again and again throughout my life to visit and work behind prison walls.

Heavyhearted, I continued my research. Many of the clergy in my counseling class and I interviewed divorced people in the church, asking, "What significant ministry did the church offer you or your children at the time of your divorce?" In all, we researched nine hundred persons. Ninety-seven percent said either they or their former spouse dropped out of the church immediately. Fifty-seven percent of those who remained changed churches or left the church within four years. Almost all said the church had no real ministry to them or to their children.

Just when singles most needed the church, the church failed them. With almost half of all adults being single, it became crystal clear why the mainline churches, begun with such evangelistic zeal for the lost and the lonely, were fading out. Only the church shoots its wounded.

Back home in Missouri, I met with John Voth, a brilliant colleague at the University of Missouri, a Ph.D. whose expertise was interpersonal communication. His wife had abandoned him and their children. He was God's man for the hour. We established a singles group called SASS (Single Adults Sharing, Serving). It grew until more than two hundred people at various times attended special get togethers "for singles only."

Patsy Kelly is an example of a person whose life was changed through this ministry. Patsy walked into Hallsville church one Sunday morning shortly after her divorce, not because she intended to be there, but because she didn't have enough gas to drive to the big church in Columbia. Like every single person who came on Sunday morning, I invited her to the parsonage for "loaves and fishes" after worship.

Loaves and fishes was born out of my own needs as a single person. It was always tough having to come home to an empty house. But on Sunday, when, like Noah's "congregation," everyone left church in pairs, that aloneness became acute.

Sundays after church had always been sacred times for our family. With the busy morning over, Sunday afternoons were spent reading the Sunday paper or playing Scrabble. Those times were like the dessert after a good meal . . . when I was married.

As a single person, each Sunday the walk to the parsonage was becoming longer and longer. So I began inviting every person who was alone to come over to the parsonage for "loaves and fishes." Whatever anyone had brought along for lunch we all shared. Sometimes I had put a roast in the oven, sometimes not. Someone would go to the store or we'd have peanut butter and crackers. But no matter how many came, we always had enough and often had some full baskets to send home.

The afternoon would be spent with Dr. Voth suggesting a word such as "Faith," "Hope," or "Love." "Tell me what it has meant to you this week." The tales that were told, the tears that were cried, the laughter that was shared could fill volumes.

SASS was not a swinging singles group, but a support group. Anyone could invite anyone to any event, and because each person paid his or her own way, nobody owed anyone anything, certainly not sexual favors. Our key verse became "Owe no man any thing, but to love one another" (Romans 13:8, KJV). And what a love group it became. They did volunteer work, painted houses for each other, helped alcoholics find Christ and lovingly cared for a man whose wife was in prison. Always paramount was the realization that Christ is the only answer to life's problems. Lives were changed and homes established.

After the first Sunday, I saw in Patsy a unique ministerial quality. I invited her to a concert the next night. We came back to the parsonage for a cup of tea which lasted until three in the morning. "You don't really want to go home, do you?" I asked as the wee hours came and I could no longer keep my eyes open.

Her plight was that of many divorced people—where to begin picking up the pieces. I visited her apartment. She had gotten half of the "stuff." It was all in boxes. It would take real courage to begin to make her half look like a whole home. I suggested she move into my guest room. She could go her way and I mine. This introduced me to a whole new concept of singleness—single pairs. She lived at the parsonage two years, leading the choir, working with John to facilitate the singles group. She wanted to pay rent; instead we built up a scholarship fund. I wept the day she moved out, but they were bittersweet tears. I would miss her, but she was going to Perkins Theological Seminary in Dallas. (She has graduated now and I am so proud of her.)

One Sunday afternoon enroute to a board meeting at Red Rock, a child, following her dog, ran into the road in front of my car. I swerved and missed the child, but my car overturned twice in a deep ravine. As I lay for weeks between life and death, Red Rock's saints of God organized prayer teams. One night I was so wracked with pain from blood poisoning that I hardly cared if I lived or died. I opened my eyes to see John Miller, tears streaming down his furrowed face, pleading with God to make me well so I could come back to Red Rock. That was the turning point. I told God that if he would just let me live and walk again I would serve him forever. Though I preached from a wheel chair for some weeks, wore a brace for several years and was never again completely without pain, I thank God for answered prayer.

With Patsy in seminary, I filled every evening with calling, meetings, friendships. Loneliness made me crowd my days with people, but in the stillness of night, thoughts of Bill came back like an avalanche.

The men at Red Rock were busy building an education unit, and Hallsville was paying off a parsonage debt I had inherited. Funds were raised by hog roasts, auctions, bake sales and tithing.

That first hog roast lasted all night. It was held at an old farmhouse. The dance band played, the whole community came—and someone brought a keg of beer. Everyone ate the hog while I wondered what to do about the beer. I ignored it and with tongues loosed, many talked of things they never would have said without that crutch. Four years later they still had hog roasts, but the beer was gone. I wonder . . . if I'd refused to attend that first evening, would the beer ever have disappeared? God doesn't clean his fish before he catches them.

The big social event in the Red Rock community was the Missouri Outlaw dances, which attracted our couples and singles alike. Loves were discovered and discarded to the tune of "Please Release Me, Let Me Go" and "The Green, Green Grass of Home." More and more of the country and western fans were coming to our social events. Some even came to our church services. Should I attend the dances? Where else could I meet so many who needed the church? As I read the life of Jesus, I concluded that he was always where the need was greatest . . . with the lepers, raising the dead, talking with the woman at the well.

I promised the new converts I would go, provided they would not abuse liquor and if they were married they would go home with their mates. They didn't always keep their promises, but as I went, the few who were "Red Rockers" increased until one whole side of the dance hall was filled with families who knew me and had some tie, however fragile, to the church.

At eleven o'clock, Ron, the lead guitarist and chairman of Red Rock's board of trustees, would announce, "Now we'll play 'Ramblin' Rose' for Dr. Rose, since she has to be in the pulpit at eight-thirty tomorrow. She's a better preacher than I am a lead guitarist. Maybe you ought to get ready to go home too, so you can find out if I'm a liar." Many took him up on the challenge. He was young, handsome, a miracle with a guitar, had a lovely wife and was searching to find a new life in Christ.

The church was being finished now . . . new steeple, foyer and educational unit, parsonage mortgage burned, Sunday school and youth groups growing. With facelifts and spirit lifts, the churches each began looking for a new organ. At Red Rock, Ron's wife, Dottie, was playing the old, out of tune piano, and some hog roast money had been set aside for the great expenditure.

Enroute to Columbia to buy the organ, she began to cry. The sun was sinking over the rim of the prairie in the red and gold sky. I stopped the car, and there, along that lonesome country road, the heart of our church was born. Dottie accepted Christ as her Lord and Savior. "I just can't play the new organ," she confessed, "unless I have that Jesus you talk about down in my heart." In the months that followed, Ron and Dot led many of the families in their band, and countless neighbors and friends, to Christ.

The enthusiasm spread to Hallsville, where packed Sunday

school classes, Well Baby Clinic and lively youth and singles groups made the community take notice. The Columbia *Tribune* ran article after article about the rebirth of the once dead churches. We began calling programs, outreach ministry, choir, nursing home and prison sharing and Bible study groups. Sunday night "guitar jamming" made the week complete.

Adding to my joy of witnessing the churches' revival was a feeling that my career was solidly on track. The Board of Ministry had told me to take leave from teaching at the college and serve four full years in order to get conference membership. Each year I had asked the college for one more year of leave. The college president had left my name on their roster, but that fourth year was the last year they could keep me on tenure and allow me to be on leave. And the fourth year was almost over.

I had served ten years in nearly closed churches. Now I longed for the same chance other faithful Methodist clergy had to work with buildings and an established congregation. Would that be possible? Bishop Handy responded with an enthusiastic "Yes," adding that there was no way he would let me leave Missouri.

But despite my happiness in answering God's call for my life, I was nevertheless lonely. Bill had been dead four years. The loneliness I felt was not from lack of friends or fellowship. Rather, it was caused by the enormous vacuum left when two great, strong men who had been husbands, lovers and confidants were gone. I had been teaching singles that "One is a whole number" and to treat themselves like someone special. I followed my own advice, and it made coming home to an empty house easier. Each night when I went out, I left soft lights on, the stereo turned to classical music or the great hymns of the church, the house clean and warm, fresh flowers and candles and hanging plants to compensate for the cheery welcome and warm body that wasn't there. Even so, some nights Haydn and Schumann were too abstract for comfort.

The weekly prison visit to Ron often left me with a despair beyond description. That Holy Presence which I had first felt on the dark night of Oscar's death had never left me. But even Jesus felt alone to the point of despair in the garden. He had needed someone human. So did I.

Since the parsonage was always filled with singles parties, youth meetings, women's groups and friends, everyone supposed I was the most unlonely woman in Hallsville. Hardly a week passed that someone who came for counseling, food or clothes did not find much more as they accepted Christ. Parties, weddings and baby showers, gospel sings, summer ball teams, swimming at the old Mill Lake and youth outings filled the days.

On Sundays at Red Rock, the Missouri Outlaw Band members and their families, dressed in jeans, sang Country Western Gospel—"I'll Fly Away" and "Turn the Radio On"—as toes tapped and hands clapped in joyous worship of their newfound faith. The congregation filled the sanctuary on Sundays and lingered long afterward.

At a luncheon on a cold, rainy April day I was introduced to Jim Sims, who was visiting from Florida. He was retired from the U.S. Air Force and an enormously creative media specialist. We chatted briefly, and then I forgot about him . . . until the phone began to ring and letters began to fill my mailbox. He had lost his wife of many years to cancer. He had loved as I had loved. I found him more interesting, with more depth and compassion for people, than anyone I had met since Bill.

He came back from Florida to see me again and we spent a day in the Amish country. We stopped at their quaint country store and bought homemade fudge. We drove by New Hope and I showed him the church. We walked silently out to the old cemetery where for twelve autumns the leaves from the great oak had covered Oscar's resting place. Twelve years is a long time. Standing there that spring afternoon, I had, for the first time, a sense of how great a healer time really is.

Jim went back to Florida. I wrote two pages in my journal that day and then forgot about him, absorbed in the many other decisions that had to be made.

7

Florida Sand in My Shoes

The college insisted that I return to teaching or relinquish my tenure. With the bishop's assurance of an appointment, conference membership finally assured and the call of God ringing with enormous clarity in my soul, I felt God leading me to leave Hallsville and Red Rock.

The district superintendent called the Red Rock and Hallsville Pastor-Parish Committee. I bought a fancy decorated cake and served it on my best china. In spite of a unanimous call from the church to remain, I sadly told them the time had come to leave.

Then I met with the District Board of Ministry, the same board which had twice before lost my records and twice changed the rules, had ordained me deacon ten years before and told me I was an associate member of the conference, only to tell me later that it was all a mistake. Now I had left no stone unturned. I had retaken the tests, served four years and completed the CPE. Finally, there was nothing they could do to deny me associate membership and an appointment. With this assurance, I had given up tenure at the college.

It had been twelve years since Bishop Goodrich had laid hands on me and I had been ordained of God. The *Discipline* says anyone who has hands laid on them by the bishop is a member of the conference, but I had not argued when the Board of Ministry said otherwise. Now, at long last, I had paid my dues in full. I could not be denied conference membership, appointment, tenure or benefits. I had been assured by Bishop Handy that I was really going to be appointed to an established church. No more closed doors or decaying buildings. No more beginning with no congregation, Sunday school, choir, youth or salary. Difficult as the decision had been to leave my beloved professorate, I knew the call of God was right for me. I was at perfect peace. What joy it would be to go to a real church with buildings waiting for me, ready to begin ministry with mature people already trained to teach, to serve on boards, to be a church.

I had always secretly longed to be a district superintendent Maybe it was not too late. I was full of ideas I wanted to share about ways to give love and encouragement to new pastors and to use psychology in the many churches that were full of conflict.

Full of anticipation, I kept my appointment with the all-male Board of Ministry. "We have decided," they informed me, "that we will not count your first year because you were not on full minimum salary at the time."

I knew I had been. I told them I would obtain proof, and I did. Both church boards gave me notarized statements testifying that I had received full salary for four years. I sighed with relief. No more hurdles. I spent a night in prayer. "Dear God, you have called me. I have served you faithfully and you have blessed me beyond my wildest expectations."

I presented the Board with the evidence and waited as they examined it. Then, rising slowly to his feet, the chairman looked me in the eye and said, "After consultation, we have decided that since you were at Harvard twenty-one days during that first year, it will not count, and you will have to do another full year."

I told them that the churches had given me an approved study leave. I pointed out that the man who served in the next town was gone from his church two months each summer to finish seminary, and that had been counted as full time. They said they were sorry. I did not make the rules, they did. Furthermore, since I was not a member of the conference and my charge was one of the strongest rural circuits in Missouri, it would have to go to someone who had conference membership. If I could find a closed church that would have me I could be appointed there.

Numbly, I walked alone to the parking lot. My call to ministry was never more clear, my future never more unclear. The presence of God had never been more real. I had all of the questions but none of the answers. I had seen fellow pastors whose churches had nearly died of neglect enjoy conference membership. Three fellow pastors, one of them on the Board of Ministry, had come to me for counseling. The pastor about whom I knew too much had come up with the Harvard stipulation. Was he uncomfortable with what he had confessed? He didn't need to be. It would never be shared.

The afternoon sun was sinking low on the crimson horizon. *Thank you, God, that the sun will come up tomorrow, no matter what today has brought.* Once again I had the feeling I'd had at Oscar's bedside. I'd never been sadder. I'd never been happier. I had no church, but I had my health. I'd had God's blessings in enormous abundance during twelve years of ministry. Three strong, vibrant, Holy Spirit-led churches had been built and filled with people whose lives had been turned around by Christ. Hitherto, God had led. I was his. All I wanted to do was serve in his vineyard. I had given God a chance to verify his call. If he didn't, I was open to new horizons. I could always write. My tenure at the college was gone, but I had earned national recognition as a school administrator. I could do it again.

Still, I felt a distinct pain and sadness, a feeling of being a minority, of my success being a threat to mediocrity. I had not asked for special favors. I had only expected to rise to the level of my competency. And I was not the only victim. Elsewhere, I saw clergy, both men and women, who faithfully preached the gospel rejected over and over again by Boards of Ministries.

Oscar's dream had been to affect the larger picture. He believed that his ministry could prove by example that with hard work, prayerful vigilance, evangelistic zeal for winning the lost, powerful preaching, willing counseling, adequate and attractive buildings and a pastor and people totally committed to Christ, any church could come alive. Souls are lost everywhere. Everyone really wants the good news that Christ died for them. Oscar wanted to prove that this vision could bring all of American Protestantism to life. The overwhelming sense that I may have failed God in Oscar's larger vision left me stunned.

I remembered a conversation I had when I approached Bishop Goodrich about full-time ministry some twelve years earlier.

"Bishop Goodrich," I had asked, "If I go into full-time ministry, is there any way I can be as much of an influence for good as I am here at the college?"

His frank answer was "No."

"Because I am not as well educated or as effective as others?"

"You have five degrees. You are one of the best educated and most effective in the state."

"Because I am a woman?"

Very reluctantly, and with great sadness, he took my hand in his. "Yes," he said.

"Bishop Goodrich," I had replied, "were I not effective in my divine call to ministry, I would not stop day or night to do his perfect will in my church. Secondly, if I were not wise enough or educated enough, I would make any sacrifice, earn any degree, study anything required to be worthy of my calling. But, to be a woman is God's divine and holy choice for me. I love being a woman. I am what I know God wants me to be, a woman with the call of God upon her life. I have never had to be masculine, aggressive, assertive or negative to be the kind of woman God would bless." With or without inclusive language, I knew I was included. If the Board of Ministry could not bless what God had already richly blessed, that was their problem.

The sun was settling low in the dusky Missouri twilight. All I could think of was that I was no closer to acceptance than when I had talked with Bishop Goodrich at the beginning of my career all those years ago.

The next Sunday Bishop Handy preached at Centrailia, ten miles away. I talked with him after the service. He listened earnestly and told me I was one of the most effective ministers he had ever seen and that a full-time church was assured. The next Monday morning, however, the district superintendent called to say, "The cabinet does not always agree with the bishop. There will be no church for you in Missouri." I asked about staying at my beloved Hallsville and Red Rock. He said there was a surplus of ministers who had conference membership, and since I did not have conference membership, my charge had already been assigned to a man who did.

My call was now being tested. I knew I was ordained of God, but Methodists had an appointment system, and I had no appointment. I could search for a closed, dilapidated church. There were plenty of them around and the Methodist church would probably appoint me to it. Or I could be more ingenious.

I spent a day in earnest prayer and fasting. Then I picked up the United Methodist *Reporter*, the national news magazine for Methodists. Fourteen jobs for associate, youth or education ministers were advertised in it. To each one I sent my resume and clippings from newspapers about my work. Thirteen replied, asking me to come for an interview.

I flew to California to investigate one of these positions. The senior pastor who met me said, "I have been told we are not here to interview you, we are here to woo you." Before the weekend was over, I had been offered the job at a figure far beyond my wildest expectations. If I accepted, I would have free reign to try to turn around the decline in this two thousand member church which had fewer in the congregation on Sunday mornings than Red Rock and Hallsville.

I seriously considered the offer until Sunday night, when the senior pastor, broken and bruised, needing someone to confide in, told me he was having an affair with his secretary. Before I left on Monday, his wife, a teacher in the public schools, also confided in me that she had been meeting a fellow teacher at a motel after school. When I met with the Pastor-Parish Committee for the final time, they could not understand how I could turn down their generous offer. But how could I serve God with sin in the camp? I firmly believe that the Methodist church is right in affirming "fidelity in marriage and celibacy in singleness." I have often been asked about alternative life-styles, especially by unsaved singles. I do not sit in judgment. When pressed for an answer, I simply say, "My own philosophy is that there is no right way to do a wrong thing." Their own experience usually leads them to the same conclusion. By then they are often ready to try Christ and walk in his way.

Two weeks later I went to Brownsville, Texas, as far south as anyone can go without leaving the United States, where I became an associate pastor. I was hired to work four days a week, and I hoped to write. But the challenge became so great that the pastor soon had me involved in calling and in singles and youth programs seven days a week, leaving little time for writing.

The most beautiful part of this ministry was meeting the lovely Hispanic people. One man especially impressed me. He was the custodian, a gracious caramel-skinned, hardworking man. His love for his family and his dedication to the church, which he lovingly polished until every corner shone, was a joy to see.

The singles ministry flourished. Soon they felt that same bond of kinship which had developed in the Missouri group. I began to see this as one of the most important ministries of the church. We went on trips together and had swimming parties. Long, lazy, sunny afternoons which could have been lonely times were filled with activities for the children and for each other.

Many a single person learned that even when all the world seemed to have turned against them, here was a place for unconditional love. To many, it provided the first honest, caring, sharing family they had ever known. Young or old, rich or poor, Spanish or white, if one hurt, we all hurt.

Some marriages always come out of this type of fellowship, but that never was a goal in our group. Our goal was for each individual to have a deep and abiding experience of new birth and newness in all their relationships. Only when that happened were they ready to begin life anew. They learned to trust again, to share, to love those hardest to love and those who were hurting the most.

At Brownsville, it was also a joy to develop a youth group with the support of truly caring parents. Too often I helped begin youth groups with little parent participation. In this organized church, however, the parents helped plan, facilitate and sponsor the youth program. We went all over Texas singing "Antselvania" on a wonderful choir tour with the kids.

It was a new experience to work with a staff and have all the luxuries of a "real" church. I was soon caught up in the excitement of ministry.

The day we returned from choir tour I had a visitor. Jim Sims, enroute from seeing his son in Kansas City to New Jersey to visit his sister, had stopped by to see me. He explained, "A trip to a friend's house is never long."

Knowing that we would never have any rest if we stayed close to the church, I took five vacation days, and we headed for a wonderful retreat ground in San Antonio. We visited the old mission, read the history of Texas' struggle for statehood and talked long and hard about our dreams.

I got to see Jim in the light of long years of separation from his wife and family. He told of spending Christmas in a Korean fox hole and his narrow escape from mortar fire when a ten-year-old boy he befriended was concealing a hand grenade. We talked of the April he returned home to his six-year-old son whom he had not seen for a year. The Christmas tree, branches bare and drooping but still decorated, and unopened gifts were waiting in faith and love for the father who might never have returned.

We prayed together. We walked the magnificent man-made canals, eating tacos and enchiladas in sidewalk cafes. Little did I know that the orchid he bought for me from a street vendor was the harbinger of a greater gift which would change my life. His was the first kindred soul I had met since death came knocking four years before.

We shared our stories, but our communication transcended mere words. He had loved deeply, then lost his beloved Ruth in a heroic battle with cancer. Their love, which had survived wars, separation, and lean times struggling to make ends meet on Air Force pay, had no weapons against cancer. He spent two years nursing her through operations and agonizing pain. In the end, when the pain had robbed her of nearly her last ounce of strength, they had said goodbye. Her last request to him was, "You have too great a capacity to love to have nowhere to spend it. When I am gone, find someone else to love."

We drove home along the beautiful Gulf of Mexico. With the moon hanging low in a mellow southern sky, I promised him I would pray for God's will for our lives.

But there was little time to think of my future when I got back. The youth minister and others had left the staff and their work load fell on me. The pastor was away on vacation.

A beautiful Catholic Spanish lady came to our church asking for burial for her Protestant husband. I asked Patty, our little Spanish secretary, to recite the rosary. I made the sign of the cross as they gently gave back to the earth her love and her life. In the quiet August afternoon, I wept silently with her.

Then, because she had no family, I invited her home. First we went to her humble room and wrapped her few possessions in a silk bandanna. She turned in her key. Her rent was up, her finances gone. Next we went to the ornate Cathedral, and I knelt with her in prayer. Then she came home with me. She stayed until I left Texas, her gracious "Buenos dias" waking me each morning as she brought steaming coffee and homemade cinnamon tarts, warm and fragrant, ministering to body and spirit.

At the end of that month I got a card from Jim. It simply said, "If you ever get Florida sand in your shoes, you will never return to Texas." He invited me to visit him in Florida. I needed some time off and asked for four days. Those four days made me certain of God's will for my life. I found a best friend, a confidant, a companion . . . better than that, I was in love again.

I had an inward fear of marrying again. Being widowed once had been painful. Being widowed twice had, except for the strength of my faith, been intolerable.

But here I was, in a relationship so deep, so tested by life's joys and sorrows, that it was a ready-made love offering from God. We called our children and told them, "We have seventy years of successful experience in marriage between us. That should count for something."

Accompanied by my Hispanic friends, I went across the Mexican border to Matamoros and returned with a floor length, white embroidered fiesta gown bought at the street market. The little Spanish children gave me a pinata. The children in Missouri broke it at our wedding, laughing and scrambling for the goodies that rained down. The church custodian, my gentle Hispanic friend whose whole life was dedicated to making God's house beautiful, gave me the finest gift of all. He and his lovely brown-eyed wife sent a homemade card, intricately painted with roses as only the Spanish can paint. It contained the message, "Those who love deeply never grow old; they may die of old age, but they die young."

Red Rock Church heard we were getting married, and declared it "unconstitutional" for us to get married anywhere else. We put a simple announcement in the bulletin at Red Rock and Hallsville:

You Are Invited to an Informal
Thanksgiving Worship Service Praising God
and Celebrating the Marriage of
Rose Grindheim Fisher and James E. Sims, Sr.
November 19, 1983
"Weeping may last for a season,
but Joy comes in the morning."

Now it was my turn to say my vows before that very altar where I had said those same words to sixty other couples. "Dearly Beloved . . ." I knew the words by heart. " . . . till death do you part."

Life is a patchwork quilt . . . love, birthdays, building, marrying, sharing, dying. Those pews had been given in memory of Bill, the piano as a memorial to Oscar. Death didn't really part. They were there in the silent reminders of the faith they had built in me, which had helped build this church. It had been worth it all, and it was worth risking again.

I shared a simple testimony. Others followed. Tears flowed. People told of lives that had been touched, hope and courage that had been rekindled, faith that had been reborn, marriages that had been reunited. Children who had been baptized were held in the arms of parents whose lives had been renewed through Jesus Christ. What a feast of love and sharing. Every pew was packed. People sat on the window ledges, children on the floor. We had been right in announcing that it would be an informal Thanksgiving service. The simple ceremony we had planned turned into nearly two hours of sharing God's love and power in the little church that had refused to let the doors stay locked.

My colleagues from the college were there also. They had often wondered why I forsook a promising academic career to go to a "God forsaken" country church. Tonight I thought they understood. All around me were more than two hundred saints of God. These friends without price had worked with me, wept with me, laughed and shared their deepest joys and sorrows with me.

The children whose parents I had married were there; all of them had been more than family to me when I was so far from my own children. How many times the children had crowded around me on the floor near the altar for that special children's time in the service which became a Sunday morning ritual. Once when I had asked the children to come forward for their story, the entire congregation decided to play a joke on me. Every single person in the church came up, crowding around the altar and sitting on the floor. Then in unison they all said, "Dr. Rose, because you led us to Christ we are all God's children."

I knew this was my final story for them. It had to be good. I opened my Bible to Genesis, read about the servant going to get a wife for Isaac. I told them God had sent a special person to me, and if they would wait and find God's will he would send just the right person for them, too. I prayed that I might say something so right that they would never forget, never make a mistake. So many of these children had already known divorce, drugs and death. I looked at Jim and thought, "Just look, kids, at what God has for those who truly wait on him." I had brought so many object lessons to them. Now Jim was the greatest object lesson of all.

Jim took the common cup. We shared our first communion together. Little did I know that soon he and I would be breaking bread together in an area so impoverished that the Tampa *Tribune* called it "America's Third World Outpost."

8

'I Was Hungry and Naked . . . and You Closed the Church'

After our wedding, we went home to Dade City, Florida, where Jim had planted his roots after serving in the U.S. Air Force for twenty-seven years. For the past several years, he had built a reputation as a skilled and caring media specialist for Adult Education students in the Pasco County Public Schools. Adult Education offers a "second chance" and in many ways his life's ministry was identical to mine. Migrants, the poor and dropouts needing a second chance never left his office without hope and courage to begin again.

I had resisted leaving rural Missouri and the land and agronomy I so loved. But to my amazement, Dade City is in the heart of rural Florida. Huge dairy farms, orange groves, pastureland and vast pine, palmetto and live oak garland every rolling hillside. Hundreds of undeveloped acres filled with cabbage palms, cypress islands and bayheads stretch between Dade City and Lakeland. I learned there are actually many Floridas. There is the Florida of manicured velvet lawns in hundreds of mobile home parks. There is also the breathtaking panorama of pine, wild orchids, spanish moss on live oaks and crimson flowered air plants.

From October to April, hundreds of retirees thumb their noses at the newscaster who describes blizzards and sub-zero temperatures in their native Canada, Michigan or New York. At last, I was one of them and loving every minute.

I should have felt no guilt at not serving a church. When Missouri had refused to give me credit for four years, they consoled me by suggesting that if I could get an out-of-state bishop to appoint me—maybe, just maybe they would consider transferring a year served elsewhere for the fourth year. As soon as they heard I was in Texas they said, "That possibility is remote."

But was I really free? Could I ever be free while America was lunging headlong into a crisis of drugs, child abuse, crime, illiteracy, illegitimacy, AIDS, broken hearts and broken hearths. We were closing churches three times faster than we were opening them. Where were the shepherds who truly tended the flocks? Who had locked them out of the pulpits and hired a hireling who came to rob and steal? Who monitored the shepherds who let half of all Sunday schools stray between 1960-1984?

Bishop Richard Wilke, in his book, *And Are We Yet Alive*, wrote, "We are sick unto death." Our beloved world was plunging headlong toward destruction of the earth, the sky, the seas and her human resources. Like many others, I was locked out of the pulpit. What if, I dreamed, every Main Street, USA had a vital country church preaching Christ, filled with the least and lost and lonely?

The call never rang louder or surer. Christ was the answer. Like Wesley, my dying breathe must lead a hurting world to him.

Yet, gentle on my mind was my call to God. I had long since learned that one is never uncalled and no paper was more precious than my ordination. I dared not let it become null and void. I wrote the Missouri Conference and asked how to keep my record alive. They said I would need to either meet with the Board of Ministry in Missouri annually or transfer my credentials and ordination to the Florida Conference.

I called the Lakeland district superintendent. He explained that Florida is teeming with ministers willing to preach. In fact, the First United Methodist Church of Lakeland had a Sunday school class of fifty persons made up solely of retired Methodist clergy. Many of these individuals would be glad to break the monotony of retirement by preaching on Sundays. Others, not retired, were available but there were no churches to give to them. I was welcome to send my credentials, he said, humoring me, "But do not count on ever serving in Florida."

I hung up the phone. The district superintendent had pronounced it loud and clear, "No church in Florida." I was free to retire.

But I longed to retire with the Methodist church winning. I knew hundreds of kindred souls who preached faithfully, won the lost and built churches. I decided to seek the bishop's guidance in setting up a trust fund which could help recapture Pentecost for the Methodist church. I knew that as long as I lived, so would the dream. If I could no longer preach, I could establish my estate as a fund for salaries for those who would pick up my mantle. My children were fairly financially independent. Jim and I made our wills. Most of my estate would go to the United Methodist Church.

If the United Methodist Church could not use my life, then surely they could use the resources God had miraculously multiplied. Long ago I had knelt and promised God my all. Like the little boy with his loaves and fishes, who with reckless abandon invested everything he had, I now stood with my twelve baskets left over. Surely God could do even more with them than he had with my original humble gift. My vision was still crystal clear. I knew it could happen anywhere.

Jim introduced me to Trilby on a Sunday pleasure drive. Just as each September I long for the smell of chalk on an ancient blackboard, I often suggested that we search out country churches as he showed me his native Florida.

Trilby United Methodist Church had had no resident pastor for fourteen years, no Sunday school for twenty, no women's work for forty. Six or eight persons attended the services in the unpainted church with a rusty tin roof. The death knell had sounded, and the conference had decided to close the church.

Lacoochee and Trilby lie just south of the Hernando County Line, just north of Dade City, Florida. Our neighbors in Dade City might be classified as being among the wealthiest in Florida . . . prosperous grove owners, cattlemen and industrialists. The palatial homes along Church Street and the subtropical climate with warm, wet summers and an average January temperature of sixty degrees make it America's ideal retirement city.

Lacoochee and Trilby lie six miles to the north—in another world. Head north on Highway 301 and you would expect to find a placid rural enclave amid rolling hills. Not far away is a magnificent state forest. The nearby Withlacoochee River flows gently into the Gulf of Mexico. Everywhere is farm country reminiscent of Missouri right down to the John Deeres and the roadside signs that read, "Hay for Sale."

The Tampa *Tribune* wrote,

> But, crossing the railroad tracks—those inevitable signposts of entry into pockets of poverty—one finds living conditions to shock the conscience of a Third World despot.
>
> The streets, where paved, are pitted with potholes and crumbling where the road meets the shoulder. Dirt-packed streets turn to mud when it rains. Standing water runs with sewage backed up in obsolete septic tanks. Children play in shirts two sizes too small and shoes three sizes too big, or none at all. They emerge from houses that any decent housing code would condemn.
>
> Bare tin roofs and windows shrouded with plastic line Market and Franklin Streets. Substandard housing that is swamped in times of flood, unsafe wiring, plugged storm drainage culverts, contaminated well water, inadequate outdoor toilets—all are blights documented from time to time by briefly interested outsiders.

In the midst of this squalor stands the former Lacoochee Methodist Church, closed since 1978. That is when, planted squarely in the middle of one of America's greatest mission fields, the United Methodist Church declared they had no mission and closed the church. They moved the non-existent congregation to Trilby United Methodist Church three miles away and sold the building for three thousand dollars. Without fanfare or funeral, in a day when ethnic minority concerns were becoming a mission priority, the door was closed and the key thrown away.

Ironically, as the Lacoochee Church declined, population in the area doubled. The modern, brick Lacoochee Elementary School, boasting six hundred multi-ethnic children, had replaced the old schools closed at Trilby and Lacoochee. But even before they moved into the new school, another extensive building program had to be planned. The population was predicted to triple in the next ten years and Pasco County was gearing for the greatest influx of people in Florida's history.

The government had built two huge low income housing projects in the area. Trailer parks and retirement communities mushroomed on the graves of frost-bitten orange groves. Every sign said, "Explosion, building, industry, tourism." Only the church failed to hear the rumblings.

Old-timers could still recall that there once were Methodist churches called Prospect, Providence, Lacoochee, Townsend and a dozen others. These now stood rotting and boarded along the Pasco County roadsides. The old Enterprise Church had been moved to the Pioneer Museum in Dade City. A historical plaque had been placed in the Trilby church, applauding the original pulpit from which the gospel of Jesus Christ would no longer be preached. How ironic! The only group that seemed to notice the church's passing was the Historical Society, but for historical reasons. Hadn't the faith of our fathers given it that historic value? Without that, the church was simply a crumbling antique. It seemed to me a museum, empty of worship and witness, would disgrace our forefathers who had sung, "Rescue the Perishing, Care for the Dying" as they built these churches.

The 1983 Christmas frost had devastated the orange groves. Eight fatal hours of below thirty degree chill had brought disaster to rural Florida and calamity for the migrant workers, grove owners and the entire economy. Where leisurely Sunday drives had once tantalized us with the fragrant aroma of orange blossoms, bare skeletons of orange trees raised their gray lifeless limbs against the torrid tropical sun.

Needy people were also struck by another tragedy. The Trilby Manor Federal Program for the Needy, which handled thousands of federal dollars, had closed because of questionable practices. The director was in prison and many who had worked with him—the poor, illiterate, innocent and guilty—were intimidated, indicted and imprisoned. Tons of commodity cheese were found hastily discarded in the lifeless groves. The story was told in national headlines.

In the midst of all this, the country churches, once bulwarks of social justice, were nailed shut, impotent, impervious to a teeming ocean of human hurt, pain, suffering and need. The mission of the church was never more needed . . . nor more absent. "I was hungry, naked and you closed the church."

Was I responsible? That was the piercing conviction of my call.

My life was singing with personal love and joy and contentment. I had never expected love to happen again, but here it was, richer and sweeter and more precious for having been without. Jim was as grateful as I for another chance.

I spent the first few months in Florida testing secret ambitions. I took a mini contract at an elementary school. Those six weeks assured me that I was still a teacher at heart. I taught courses at St. Leo College, Divorce Recovery seminar at the Holiday Inn in Tampa and a Death Recovery seminar at the junior college. I delighted in cooking gourmet dinners for two, complete with candlelight and roses. The melodies of Schumann, Schubert and the Wesleys blended with the joyous song of life renewed.

Subconsciously, I closed the door in my beautiful home and, just for this once, lived untouched by those in need. If the district superintendent was right, the Florida Conference had an ample surplus of male clergy ready and willing to meet every human and spiritual need. Thus, the six miles to Trilby became like six thousand. The long, lonely, fifteen-hour days of opening churches were over for me. My life had for so many years been on hold. Furthermore, I emphatically told myself, serving another church had not been in the contract when Jim had asked me to marry him.

Living in Florida was like a daily Disney World. I could see why the highways were crowded with a thousand new citizens moving here every week. The sun always shone, the beaches were crystal clear and camellias, gardenias and azaleas bloomed in profusion all year. Jim had every weekend free. Clad in shorts and matching tee shirts, we headed for the beaches as soon as he got home on Fridays. What a far cry this was from the leaner years both of us had known living our lives close to the battle zones.

Never again would I spend nights praying and planning for a new church roof, new pews or an organ. And no more parsonages;

this house was *my* house. I could spend whatever I wished, without guilt that the apportionments weren't paid or that we needed a home for a single parent who would otherwise be a street person. Once Oscar and I spent three years in a master bedroom a former pastor had papered with cowboys and Indians for his son. The paper had been new and we did not want to ask the church for permission to change it. Now I reveled in a house that did not require trustee approval to change the wallpaper.

Then one day the phone rang. It was the district superintendent who had my records in hand. He read what had happened during my four decades of opening closed churches. He was on his way to close Trilby.

"Would you be willing to open it?"

"No, you have plenty of pastors who can do that."

He asked if we would come to Trilby to hear him preach. We said, "Yes."

A tiny handful of people stumbled through the familiar hymns from the old brown Cokesbury hymnal and listened to the district superintendent's brief sermon. Then, to fewer souls than you could count on your hand, he began reading my clergy work record for the past twelve years. He quoted articles in national and state papers describing the success of New Hope, Hallsville and Red Rock. Then to my utter amazement, he said, "How would you like this women to be your pastor? She is the lady sitting on the back bench." I was stunned that he would do this without asking me. I was amazed at the attempt to manipulate me into a job which not one of the crowd of retirees was willing to tackle. We invited the D.S. back to our home for lunch, and I repeated my emphatic "*No.*" Our suitcases were already packed for Jim's summer vacation.

The next six weeks we lazed our way up eight thousand miles of the Eastern seaboard, marveling at the miracle that is America.

It was a family time with leisure to renew the enormous love I had for my precious grandchildren, Ben and Ann, and to meet each other's families. From the Pennsylvania Dutch country to the waving wheat fields of Kansas, we wandered like gypsies. I had no responsibility for substitute speakers at a church, no building projects ahead, nothing but an eternity left to love and live in the luxury of life's task complete.

Admittedly, we visited every little country church we found, took pictures and visualized what they could become. On Sundays we sat in half-empty pews while memories drowned out the sermon. It was on such a visit that a soloist touched my heart and soul with her rendition of "God's Not Through Using You." The song kept ringing in my heart as we wended our way home.

On some sleepless, prayer-filled nights I would be tempted to go to Trilby. The D.S. had said I would only have to give them an hour a week. In return, they would give me as salary the $125 a month rent they got from the old, unpainted ghetto parsonage.

I knew the offer was ludicrous. I had never taken a church to officiate at its demise. Dying churches need intensive care. But, I rationalized, crime, murder, drugs, alcohol and poverty made it unsafe to be there at night. Besides, I now wanted to put all of my energies into this great new marriage, teach a little at the college and enjoy retirement. The multitude of ministers in Florida could try to open Trilby.

St. Leo College had asked me to teach, and I decided to accept.

But everything changed on an August day in 1984. Enroute to sign my contract at St. Leo College, I stopped by Jim's office.

"Tear it up," he laughed, "and sit down and write what I dictate."

I sat down, thinking it was a joke.

"Write and tell them you are going to Trilby and won't be teaching this fall."

He was dead serious. That was the sign I needed. This man who had spent his life in the military had now enlisted us both in God's army. I asked him if he knew the price we would have to pay and was he willing to pay it? What would it do to our marriage? Our finances? Our weekends? The Midwest farm crisis had reached me too. That income was gone. Jim worked all week. I would be busy all Sunday.

"Rose," he proffered, "God called me to marry you. I knew you were a minister. Let's get going." Never once has he faltered on that call. No minister's spouse in all the world could be more faithful, more sustaining and supportive. Yes, I would go to Trilby.

9

The Most Precious Antique of All

I went home and got on my knees. Of every mountain peak I had ever climbed for God, truly this was transfiguration. Tears of joy flooded my soul and once again I sensed the Divine overshadowing Presence. Yes, Oscar's mantle was doggedly in place. Only now where once it had seemed awkward and heavy, it was a well-worn yoke. In surrender and dedication I knew in faith's eye that finally I would be able to declare to an America teetering on the point of no return: "It can happen anywhere." What a gift Jim had given to me.

I made some phone calls. I would take Trilby . . . but wanted every day to count toward conference membership. The D.S. assured me it would. He later called to say the cabinet had arbitrarily grandmothered me in as a local pastor with deacon's orders. To make sure this had happened, I asked to meet with the Board of Ministry, but the D.S. assured me it was not necessary.

Then, without a single doubt about God's will for my life, I drove my car six miles north, singing all the way, to the world of unparalleled crime, poverty and despair I had tried in vain to ignore.

The morning paper featured a story about Trilby and Lacoochee entitled, "The shameful blindness that keeps the destitute out of sight." The article explained how "These people do not know what a bathtub is. When the houses were built forty years ago, you put a shovel in the ground and you had water. The septic tanks are almost on top of the ground and on warm days the stench is suffocating. This abandoned mill town teems with teenagers deep into crime and drugs, barefoot babies having babies, people so poverty stricken and ignored that they are a societal blight beyond endurance."

Now, this had become my parish. Spanish moss draped itself lazily on every live oak. The Withlacoochee River was redundant with fisherman pulling out catfish and grouper. I, too, was a fisherman.

Jim had told me it was not safe to be in Trilby at night, but this was daytime. Wild purple phlox painted the countryside and pennyroyal's hairy sepals scented the summer air. Majestic live oak encircled the church. I hummed "There's a Church in the Valley by the Wildwood" softly under my breath. I was not being foolhardy. I knew exactly what lay ahead, yet a "peace that passes all understanding" overwhelmed me.

Trilby is one of those multi-ethnic, unincorporated one-horse towns. As I approached the church, I heard God giving marching orders. "Now then, you and all these people, get ready to cross the Jordan River into the land I am about to give to them. . . . I will give you every place where you set your foot, as I promised Moses" (Joshua 1:2-3).

Taking off my shoes, tears of joy flooding my soul, faith singing in my heart, I firmly set foot on Trilby's promised land. I began at the corner of Old Trilby Road and County Road 575 where the ninety-year-old forgotten church cast its shadow across the fly-infested mud hole that would one day be a prayer garden replete with roses. At that very corner, the weedgrown stubble and briars piercing my shoeless feet, I staked my claim for God.

"The Lord your God has given you the land. Go up and take possession of it as the Lord . . . told you. Do not be afraid; do not be discouraged" (Deuteronomy 1:21). The sun was sinking in the crimson tropical sky, casting shadows across the horrendous old extension building that housed the "one seater" the church had used as an excuse for not putting up a proper outhouse.

Oscar had never once in his ministry seen an empty church.

Now, with vivid clarity, my faith's eye saw this house of God packed to capacity with singles, children, adults of every race, every strata, every gender. Kneeling in the shadow of that old weatherworn, termite-ridden, unpainted house of God, I lifted my heart skyward and thanked God that my call had led me to this holy ground.

"Whatsoever ye ask in faith, believe ye have." Was it blind faith? No, "Hitherto the Lord hath led." I dared not doubt a God who had already proven himself during nearly forty years of ministry. God had not failed even once to keep his promises.

Night falls without warning in the tropics. My prayer was over, my commitment was made, my course was set. The scarlet sky had turned to pitch black and the stars were coming out. When I arrived home, Jim's concern for my safety in that troubled area was evident but overshadowed by a strange glow.

"You had a phone call," he said. "The student who bought your farm called to say his wife's grandmother, who is eighty-five, doesn't think he should be paying twelve percent interest. She wants to pay the farm off in cash. Would that be okay?"

"Before they call I will answer" (Isaiah 65:24).

Was it okay? Amen! Now I had money I had earned before my marriage that could be given without the guilt of spending Jim's hard-earned investments. At that time, I did not realize the depth of Jim's faith and vision. Through the next four years, his investment of faith, courage and finances always far exceeded mine.

God could have let us have cash in hand before we in faith accepted Trilby, but he didn't. "Bring the whole tithe into the storehouse. . . . Test me in this . . . and see if I will not throw open the floodgates of heaven and pour out so much blessing that you will not have room enough for it" (Malachi 3:10).

Jim and I sat down at the kitchen table and started figuring what we would need to get started . . . a reliable car, a typewriter, a copy machine, a computer, telephones, funds for advertising, a desk, file, office space. Our lovely home in Dade City was just six miles away and would become the parsonage. The spare bedroom (with new office furniture) would for now make an office for counseling and ministry.

In one brief decision, Jim had become one of Florida's finest minister's spouses. "You'll need to get the old church roof painted first, then we'll tackle the walls." The trumpets of God were blaring now, loud and clear. Jim had heard them first.

When he married me it had never been a part of the package that I would become a pastor again, much less serve in this destitute, devastated mission field. Here we were with unlimited retirement options and he was choosing *me and Trilby*.

I seldom preach about giving. Nor do I ever guarantee anyone that serving God will make him rich. I can only say "No eye has seen, no ear has heard, no mind has conceived what God has prepared for those who love him" (1 Corinthians 2:9).

The world is astonished at what God can do through people who are wholly dedicated to him. In those midnight hours Jim and I, frail and faltering, but filled with his Holy Spirit, committed our lives to trying to be two such people.

By comparison, my early days in ministry had been lean, with someone always going to school. But God had always proven himself, even when we failed.

Every parsonage has its own bit of humor. Our favorite parsonage story came from our days in drought stricken Octavia, Nebraska. Oscar was in graduate school. We fervently prayed the three thousand dollar a year salary would stretch from pay day to pay day, from semester to semester.

One day the mortician called to ask Oscar to preach a funeral. A stranger with no living relatives had requested that his body be shipped from Texas to be buried under the mighty oaks in the ancestral plot in the shadow of our church.

Usually funerals were times of grief for all of us since country folks become families. But nobody knew this man. Afterwards the mortician handed Oscar a check for twenty-five dollars, an unheard of honorarium in those days. Oscar never felt he should take money for funerals from church families. After all, he was called to help in both joy and sorrow. But this time Oscar said, "This is money God sent as a special love offering to us. It is money we never planned to have, and it has been months since we have celebrated, so let's all get dressed up and go to Omaha." Peals of laughter rang through the old rambling country parsonage. The twenty-five dollars might as well have been a million.

Octavia, population one hundred, boasted one store, Stibals

General Mercantile. (The girls had nicknamed it "The Three Wonders" . . . Wonder if he has it? Wonder if he can find it? Wonder if we can afford it?) Stibals was gas station, post office, hardware, grocer, dime store and general information center. We stopped there for gas on our way to Omaha. The mail truck was just pulling in and everyone had gathered to wait for the mail and to swap stories.

Gaylie, our kindergartner, was utterly amazed that we had money for just plain celebrating. As Stibal pumped the gas, she rolled down the window and at the top of her lungs informed those gathered for the day's gossip, "Guess what? We're out celebrating 'cause somebody died!"

Yes, God is also Lord of our finances. He was answering our prayers for Trilby even before we prayed them.

Our first task was to make the church attractive and inviting so that people would want to attend. I contacted the bishop, who called Rev. Dean Witten, the product of a little country church now defunct, who was pastor at the United Methodist Temple in Lakeland. Accompanied by a professional painter, they set out to "view the land." Their verdict was that the walls could be painted but nothing could be done with the rusty tin roof.

I learned that $1,400 of the $3,000 from the old Lacoochee church had been hoarded in the Trilby treasury. As with every vote we have taken since, the vote to release the funds if I could find a painter was unanimous. I prayed for a miracle, but nobody would tackle the job. Then I heard of a Catholic painter who would attempt it for $3,000, but would offer no guarantee that it would succeed. We offered him $1,400. We would have to professionally wash the roof first. Jim, with his usual foresight, invested in washing both the roof and the church.

The painter must have lost money. He scraped and cleaned and painted the roof with two coats of brilliant scarlet. We wanted the world to see that the sleepy little Trilby church was waking up, yawning and stretching.

When he was through, the old tin roof shone in the sunlight like a ragamuffin waif who had fallen heir to a new tee-shirt but had forgotten to beg a substitute for his tattered pants.

Astounded, the Lakeland church offered to come and help paint.

Three Saturdays, a work crew, newspaper publicity and dinners served by the ladies, and our church was on the map.

My study of statistics had taught me how to analyze covariance. If you have three groups, one undergoing a treatment you have proven effective, another with a different kind of treatment and a third receiving no treatment, you have the makings of a research study.

If the sample group undergoing the special treatment consistently tests as having a statistically significant difference, then you can rely on getting the same results every time you apply the special treatment. In statistics that is called "reliability." I wanted to prove reliable church growth.

"Variables" are those things which make each situation unique and different. They are often called "confounding variables." These "confounding variables" make a D.S. say, "It may have happened in Nebraska but it can't happen in Florida. It may happen in a declining rural church but not in an urban area. It will happen when Rose is there but not when we change leadership. It can't happen where there has been a split, or they are in debt."

True, no two declining churches are alike. However, our ministry was fraught with confounding variables . . . the drought-ridden Nebraska church where they had not taken their corn pickers into the fields for four years, the Seattle church killed by internal strife, the Ohio church hit by the farm crisis which caused land values to plummet. At Anaconda the copper smelter was closing. In Octavia, Nebraska, a court battle between two members had ended with one member dying of heart failure during the trial.

Yet each of these unidentical churches had become one of the first in its state in the professions of faith ratio, built debt-free buildings, paid apportionments in advance and filled the sanctuary with the lost and the lonely.

Researchers would ask, "What are the constants? Faith and determination?" I was naive enough to believe that the answer is even simpler than that. The call to ministry is "go and make disciples of all nations." If the church is empty, there must be lots of people outside needing Christ.

If Oscar had hit on a winning formula, couldn't it be written up so that others could replicate it? In the back of my mind, however, I knew that there would have to be two other ingredients before others could use his "recipe."

First, the denomination leaders would have to believe that "it can happen anywhere and it must happen everywhere" and affirm this belief with their finances. A hospital doesn't allocate its second-best doctor and resources to the intensive care ward. Secondly, competent, biblically-oriented, evangelical ministers who have met every requirement for ordination and conference membership must receive justice.

A minister's competency must be considered as a part of his or her evaluation for membership, regardless of the minister's gender or evangelical zeal. And, on the other side of the coin, incompetency must not be rewarded.

We must find some positive answer to the terrible twenty-four-year decline of the United Methodist Church. (See Wilke, *And Are We Yet Alive*.) Trilby was more than just one more little church. It was one more God-given chance to tell America's churches that it can happen anywhere .

Without further delay, we rolled up our sleeves and went to work as if the ministry were a life and death matter, which indeed it is. "Whoever believes in the Son has eternal life, but whoever rejects the Son will not see life, for God's wrath remains on him" (John 3:36).

Evangelism Explosion and most other evangelism programs suggest that we get around to asking two questions which pinpoint every person's greatest need: (1) Have you come to the place in your spiritual life that you know for certain you have eternal life? (2) Suppose you were to die tonight and God were to say to you, "Why should I let you into my heaven?" What would you say?

Before the roof was painted we began asking those questions. God did not call us to convert the world but to make disciples. If every pastor won ten souls to Christ daily, at his death the population explosion would leave more lost than saved. But if he trains every convert to win ten more and each new convert wins ten more, the world could be won in our lifetime. No one is more enthusiastic than a brand new Christian. Soon, like Andrew of old, each would bring brothers and sisters to meet the Savior.

But how do people find out where to go for answers to the deepest questions of their lives? We must tell them. Industry would die if it did not advertise. No church can grow until it sells itself to the community. Once it does that, it can "Offer them Christ." Almost every Missourian had known about New Hope, Hallsville and Red Rock. Now Florida must know about Trilby.

Every Sunday I laboriously wrote next Sunday's notices for every paper in the area. I called the newspapers, the television and radio stations. I asked reporters to cover special events. Ministers fail to do this for two reasons: (1) It is terribly time consuming, and (2) they might be criticized as egotists.

How long would Kellog's corn flakes last if nobody bragged about them? But in the final analysis, advertising is fruitless if the final product does not live up to its claim. The Trilby church, the people who came and accepted Christ, had an electrifying enthusiasm. True, the days were long, the days off nonexistent. But I remembered my daughter and her husband during their medical residency. It is expected that those who dedicate their lives to the critically ill and dying count lives saved, not hours spent.

Wesley had said, "Offer them Christ." Two hundred years later we used the same formula and it still worked.

It had been only a few short weeks since I left Texas and now I was in the pulpit again. My first sermon to the tiny congregation had ten two-letter words. "If it is to be, it is up to me." I preached about the man at the pool of Bethesda and asked, "Do you want to get well?" Did the man at the pool want to get well? Surely one of those friends who faithfully brought him would have stayed long enough to get him to the healing waters. But if he got well he would have to pick up his bed and get busy helping others into the healing waters. He would have to deal with sickness, need and apathy.

The organist, Miriam Pire, had undergone a mastectomy five years before. Now she had cancer of the bone marrow that left her scarcely able to climb the organ bench with the help of a walker. Another member, Bob Long, was in the hospital with terminal lung cancer. The third old-timer, seventy-year-old Cliff Couey, rose to pray. Tears choked his barely audible prayer: "God, I joined this church fifty-five years ago. Please help Miriam and Bob. You know we don't have two members to lose."

Miriam went back to the doctor. He said he could see where the bone cancer had left scars but could find no trace of it. She played our organ for the next four years, not without some pain and treatments, but always with a faith that was contagious. Bob also surprised the doctors the next week when they declared him well enough to go home. He is still with us.

That experience made Clifford my prayer partner. Truly "more things are wrought by prayer than this world dreams of." I don't know as much as I would like to know about divine healing. I have stood by so many in pain and felt so inadequate. But I do know about prayer. Clifford has spent full time in prayer these last four years, reading the Bible through time after time and calling me to say he is praying day and night for me.

If a church is to grow, enlist prayer partners. Building country churches is not just a matter of technical know-how. We are engaged in spiritual warfare. It is imperative to enlist the saints and identify the enemy.

We did everything we could think of to let people know our church is there for them.

When I spied an empty billboard, I called the owners with an offer they couldn't refuse: "I would like to offer you the opportunity to do something significant that will last for eternity." We paid $250 for the painting. In return, we had free use of a huge illuminated billboard on Highway 301.

I had taken every course on marketing I knew of and learned that yellow and black is best on a billboard and that a secular symbol will attract attention faster than a sacred one. Our enormous yellow and black sign features a fluffy baby chick breaking out of its egg and reads, "Begin life anew at Trilby United Methodist Church." Six million cars pass by each month. Since then we have added several other bulletin boards on the highway.

And of course, we have a beautiful new church sign articulating the time of service and pastor's name. It stands in a planter abloom with geraniums and petunias. The ten-foot cross and flame let folks know that we are United Methodist. Nobody can come near Trilby without being aware that we are, "Thank you, alive and well." One sees so many shabby, untended, unpainted invitations to the work of the King of Kings.

I began calling the very first Monday morning. My first counselee was a sixty-seven-year-old ex-convict who wanted me to marry him to a mentally retarded teenager. The second call was on the teenager we had to get to safety. Nobody said life was going to be easy!

The second day I spent volunteering at the commodity food give away. I asked how many elderly or handicapped people could not come to the site and offered to take the food to them. It was late that night before I got home. I had visited homes so impoverished they compared with those in third world countries. A Health Department study verified that our area had fourteen percent of the communicable diseases although it contained only three percent of the county's population.

During the next four years, ninety-five percent of the youth who came to youth fellowship lived with only one biological parent. Our food program, coupled with the minimum wage most of their parents earned, helped keep many off welfare. Our "Thank God it's Friday" get together for singles always ended with huge boxes of food available anonymously to all whose budget needed easing.

As I worked in the community, I discovered that everything I heard about this area was true. Homes had no running water, many homes were windowless and devoid of a floor. Bathrooms were a rarity. Swarms of mosquitoes and flies bothered me far less than the cockroaches which seemed large enough to saddle and ride. They scurried from every garbage strewn street, under the porches and over the baby cribs. All this existed six miles from my home surrounded by millionaires.

But the people who lived in the rapidly multiplying trailer parks needed Jesus just as much as those in the poorest homes. To reach them, I contacted RV park owners. Would they like to have sing-alongs in the parks? Did their tenants have food or clothes they would like to donate? Travelers' Rest, an Airstream Park managed by Paul Ruth, a devoted Christian, made appeals. People began asking how they could help. Those who read our story in the newspaper came to worship with us, bringing food and clothes. Door-to-door calling paid off and these people began to help fill the church.

A newsletter proclaimed the virtues of the old-fashioned country church: "Why pay a fortune for antiques and abandon the most priceless antique of all . . . the ninety year old revived Trilby United Methodist Church?" and "Lonesome for that honest, old-fashioned caring of the little country church back home? Worship with us on Sunday."

In a few short weeks it was time for a harvest festival. For the occasion we invited the D.S. to conduct our charge conference. More than two hundred persons crowded into the church with a seating capacity for eighty. We had to borrow chairs and tables from the Masonic Lodge. The bountiful turkey dinner was supplemented with covered dishes, salads, pies and cakes—the love offerings of country parishes. When we ran out of tables and chairs, blankets were spread on the lawn.

Trilby had the first traffic jam in its history. The highway patrol came by to say we must hire an off-duty policeman if we ever planned to do this again. (I thought, "We do! We do!" but didn't say it aloud.) Parking was a problem from that day on, but what a nice problem. The most amazed person was the district superintendent who just a few short weeks ago had come to close the church.

The trailer park residents brought van loads of food and clothing. These gifts forced those who brought them to get out and visit the recipients. One women had been saving her son's baby things for the day he had a son of his own, but gave them all away to a new mother whose baby did not have even a diaper. Homes that had no windows found men who knew where they could at least get some screens. Teenagers who were dropping out of school found new dignity in recycled clothes. Many of these teenagers took Jim's advice, wore their new clothes, and went back to school to get their GED.

We sang the old-fashioned hymns: "Lord send the old-time power, the Pentecostal power." And, like the early church, when people spoke in the understandable tongues of the people, love, evangelism and caring, "Everyone was filled with awe, and many wonders and miraculous signs were done" (Acts 2:43).

Six weeks before, it would have been foolhardy to talk about building. Now the conference offered us a loan, which we turned down. We tried never to build with borrowed money. But, we had attracted the attention of the Florida Conference. When I asked for a ten thousand dollar grant and received it, Trilby was on its way.

At Christmas the youth packed the church with a party for the needy. Keith Pire cut a ceiling-high pine tree. We sang carols in the nursing homes and door-to-door, to the poor and forgotten and to the rich and often equally lonesome. The church was a veritable beehive with saints and sinners alike coming to either give or receive.

If built by a contractor, the new church would cost at least three hundred thousand dollars. We had ten thousand dollars and one builder when we broke ground. God had let us all "stand in wonder and awe" as one miracle after another brought Pentecost to Trilby. I knew that if we were faithful, if we worked as if it were a life and death matter, God could multiply that ten thousand dollars into buildings worth close to half a million and fill them to capacity.

Our first big hurdle was to find a certified Florida contractor to sign our plans. That poses an enormous risk to a contractor, who must assume an awesome responsibility. We would also need to recruit a vast army of volunteers; without them we could never build. I spent the summer speaking and making appeals to larger churches. Many large churches need the spark of a mission project to ignite their own growth.

Zephyrhills UMC sent their associate pastor, Ann Gadbolt, as well as a van full of youth who packed every corner of the church for our first Day Camp. Youth from Trilby got caught up in the spirit and our first youth fellowship, with sixteen converts, became the core of evangelism in Trilby.

Years of experience had taught me that missions and evangelism must be number one priorities. I suggested that before we even touched the ten thousand dollar grant for a new church, we should build a mission. We needed a place to distribute clothes and food. The many babies in our area needed a clean, attractive WIC (a nutrition program for women, infants and children) and Well Baby Clinic. The vote was unanimous. Everything else would be put on hold. Converting the old parsonage seemed an ideal temporary solution. "But," said that handful of members reluctantly, "the $125 a month rent has been our only source of reliable income for the last fourteen years. It has paid an itinerant preacher to come and preach on Sunday mornings. Could we do without the parsonage rent?" I listened to those faithful few and was deeply troubled. I had taken the church, knowing I could not count on the salary to cover even car expenses, but someday my mantle would fall on others less financially able to serve but equally called of God.

If the Methodist church did not see a need for a salary for those called to God's byways, who would continue to carry the dream?

This dilemma gave birth to an idea. We could designate our estate in a fund to help other ministers open closed churches.

Perhaps some churches die because they get pastors who use the church as a stepping stone until something bigger and better comes along or until they retire. This is like drinking the priming water, eating the seed potatoes or burning the siding of the house to keep warm. What would happen if we sent our best pastors and greatest resources for those churches nearest death? What would happen if we rewarded competency and made success in a small church a criteria for advancement? To that end, we established the Grindheim-Sims award in the Florida Conference. This annual award will honor Oscar's dream and his life, and express my heartfelt thanks to Jim for being, in my admittedly biased opinion, Florida's finest minister's spouse.

Our house served as both parsonage and church office. Soon it was filled with those who needed counseling, help and Christ. Jim had bought me a new typewriter, computer and copy machine, and installed a church phone. These were an absolute necessity to our new work, but I saw them as stumbling blocks to my dream. Resurrection has a price many churches could not afford to pay. Jim's salary was paying the utilities, parsonage and local and long distance phone calls. In those first three years the new car covered every highway and byway. Each time the gas gauge registered empty it was mysteriously and lovingly filled and serviced. These were "confounding variables" that would be hard for many who would follow to replicate.

I knew that if my work was to become a pilot project for other closed churches, I would have to get the attention of the United Methodist Church so that it would be willing to ensure that other pastors would not have to risk their life savings. Could I in my lifetime get America to see that "it can happen anywhere and must happen everywhere"? It would be a tough, lonely, lifelong battle, one that Oscar had not won. The dream would come true when evangelical pastors with compelling vision could be given salary, parsonage, conference membership and the same amount of funds ordinarily given to new extension churches.

Once that is accomplished, the "endangered species"—the sixty percent of Methodist churches with fewer than seventy-five people in Sunday school—could be revitalized.

10

Magic Oranges

Trilby became a people-oriented church in a thousand little ways. For example, the church helped the family who occupied the old parsonage find a new and better house when the parsonage was converted into a mission. Shirley, the mother, later accepted Christ, joined the church and was one of the first of our singles to be married in our new church.

In a people-oriented church, everyone matters. As I sit here today writing, a meaningful interruption has netted employment for a Hispanic farm worker family with seven beautiful children. As migrant farmers following the onions, pickles and oranges, their only housing has been a crew leader's house, which meant, "I owe my soul to the company store." A phone call and letter of introduction, and he has a job as nursery caretaker at an elite country resort. A phone call to the right people at HUD and a four bedroom house is assured, if he has a job. Mission accomplished. But then the phone rings again. HUD rules say no more than eight people may live in a four bedroom house. A few calls are made, a letter written to plead their case. I don't know how it will turn out. I grew up in an immigrant family with nine children. I was born in a four room house. My mother hung hammocks over the beds and put the ones who were potty trained up there for obvious reasons.

Multi-ethnic ministry was a missionizing priority in our conference. I realized that Trilby's needs were too staggering for us to handle alone. I thought I had seen poverty overseas. I had written my doctoral dissertation on "A Comparative Study of Head Start Programs" and was certain I had seen it all. But this poverty was mind boggling. I applied to the Board of Global Ministries for a multi-ethnic grant and learned I could get one if I were a black pastor. I had often been told I was the wrong sex. Now I was the wrong color. However, we eventually did receive five thousand dollars from the Ethnic Fund and a ten thousand dollar grant from the Board of Global Ministriesto equip and finish the mission.

The Dade City Methodists gave us a forty-four passenger bus they were not using. The next week we had a Kids' Krusade attended by two hundred children, most of whom were Hispanic or black. We asked the United Methodist Publishing Board to declare us a new church. They did, and we got free bulletins and Sunday school materials for a whole year. I applied for the Livingstone Mission Fund which was left as a trust to build new churches, but we were turned down because we were not a "new work." (Another confounding variable.) We knew we had to make the conference declare closed churches as "extension churches" so they could get equal justice.

All this the bishop needed to hear. If he would dedicate the mission, we might become an Advanced Special. He might be able to enlist other churches to share in our outreach.

I did not sleep that Sunday night. Early Monday morning I posed the ridiculous idea to Jim that "Bishop Earl Hunt is just the person to see our mission and dedicate it."

Jim wasn't awake yet and was sure he must be dreaming. "The bishop is booked years in advance. Why don't you ask the district superintendent?"

"Because we need the bishop. Besides, it is just as easy to ask God for a bishop as a district superintendent."

I knew before I picked up the phone that this holy hunch was an absurd request. No bishop was more beloved by his people, or more in demand.

His secretary said he was in Atlanta. I should have given up then and there. I asked where he was staying and called his hotel.

"Bishop Hunt, I am Rose Sims. I know it is presumptuous, but we need you to dedicate our mission." I told him of our neighborhood and our church's outreach to the lost and the lonely.

Before he hung up he had cancelled his next Sunday's speaking engagement and promised to be with us.

Armed with the news of the bishop's coming, the entire community was mobilized. The press, television and radio stations were alerted. A newsletter went out far and wide. Volunteers worked night and day.

The mission was finished and resplendent with garden flowers, the yard manicured. The freshly painted old church was abuzz with activity. Borrowed tables were spread on every grassy inch of church property. Kitchens bustled with laity preparing for a country eatin' meetin' worthy of the Florida bishop.

It was the first time in ninety years that a bishop had come to Trilby. The St. Peter *Times* and the Tampa *Tribune* carried front page stories. The Trilby people won the hearts of the Florida Conference. Everywhere I spoke someone volunteered to help.

Almost every Sunday someone had come to the altar to accept Christ. The baptismal waters were stirred. Every new convert wanted to use his or her talents. A volunteer choir composed of new Christians belted out the old songs with gusto, but we desperately needed a choir director. Our church was learning that "If you believe, you will receive whatever you ask for in prayer" (Matthew 21:22).

Sometime later, Phil Austin, an outstanding former director of the Ticonderoga, New York, High School Music Department, heard me speak. He was eighty going on twenty. It was a turning point for our church when he walked into our faltering choir rehearsal and said, "I believe the Holy Spirit has asked me to direct your choir, and I have asked him for a balanced choir of twenty voices." That was a tall order, but the next week God gave him exactly what he'd asked for—twenty voices able to sing all four parts. Phil was not only a magnificent minister of music; he was a mature Christian whose wise counsel and warm friendship made him confidant to the entire church. He brought his son, Norm, a retired member of the

Annapolis Navy Band. In eternity, Gabriel's trumpet won't sound sweeter.

Everything at Trilby United Methodist Church seemed to be rolling full-steam ahead, but one more thing had to happen before we were ready to build. Methodists annually assign each church apportionments which are used for world-wide missions. Apportionments declare that "The world is our parish." Churches wrapped up tightly in themselves soon become such a small package that they choke and die. No church can survive which has tunnel vision. After all, Jesus commissioned us to "go and make disciples of all nations" (Matthew 28:19). This meant that if Trilby were to enjoy real growth, we must pay our debts before we bought anything new for ourselves. "It's like buying a fur coat when you owe the grocer," Oscar had always said.

But the church treasury was empty, and Jim and I had exhausted his December paycheck. Nevertheless, we began a practice I had found to be effective over the years. We paid our apportionments in full in advance of January 1. It wasn't easy. Human need at home in Trilby was so paramount. But, like the widow's cruse, once the cruse is emptied for God the oil never ceases. Once done, it becomes habit. I believe that if the United Methodist Church could learn to do this, the interest from the amount given in apportionments could help change the tide for the church. Today Trilby never asks about apportionments. We expect to be among first in the state to pay them. The strange thing is that, having done so, we never talk about money, nor need to. All we talk about is commitment.

Spring came. Although nobody would hire me when I first came to Florida, I now had several offers. I was bargaining from a position of strength. Realizing any pastor who followed me would need a salary, I insisted I would not accept reappointment to Trilby if I were not put on full minimum salary. I reminded the conference again, and they assured me they understood, that I was a full-time deacon serving under my second appointment in Florida.

By October it was time to build. Allen Cole, owner of Seven Acre Park, promised to let us use his earth-moving equipment on Saturday, when it was idle at the park, to dig the footings. Keith Pire was the only member able to help with the building project as a full-time volunteer. We found a local contractor who said he would sign our plans. It was Thursday. The plans had to be signed that night so they could be taken to the building inspector on Friday, allowing us to dig on Saturday. Keith and I went to the local contractor's house and stood under a giant pecan tree in the rain, waiting for him to come home to sign our permit.

He never came. Eventually his wife came out to say she had persuaded him that it was too dangerous to risk his Florida contractor's license by signing his name to a building project that would use only volunteers. Who were we to think we could build a church with no men, no money, no contractor? She was right. But I knew something she didn't: One layperson and God are a majority. A bishop once said in introducing me, "Everybody said nothing could be done at Trilby. The problem is, we forgot to tell anyone at Trilby."

The ominous clouds loomed black as midnight as the sky pelted us with driving rain. Florida is America's worst lightning country, so we sought shelter in Keith's pickup. There one drenched preacher and one lone layman called on the almighty God of wind and storm. Keith prayed a simple prayer, asking God for a contractor.

As if his "Amen" heralded the dawn, sunshine pierced the clouds and broke in splendor over the evening sky. Keith and I both saw it at the same time. A brilliant rainbow spanned the horizon end to end. It was all the encouragement we needed. God would somehow, in the next twelve hours, perform a miracle and send us a contractor to sign our permit.

Jim suggested I call the district superintendent or the bishop. I did, but neither of them knew of any Methodist contractors who might sign the permit. It was now ten o'clock at night.

I knew for certain that by morning we would have a signature, but whose? I paged through my address book. I had become a popular speaker for men's organizations' banquets and church growth seminars.

Somewhere, while speaking, I am not certain where, I had jotted down a name. There it was, scribbled almost illegibly: Roland Strnad, Contractor. It was now ten-thirty and he would probably be in bed, but I called anyway. This dedicated owner of Cypress Construction Company and member of St. John's United Methodist Church in Winter Haven had led missions to Honduras and Haiti to build churches.

"You bet I'll sign your contract," he responded to my plea.

"Tonight?"

"Tonight."

It was an hour's drive to Winter Haven. Jim went with me. At midnight the contract was signed. By two-thirty we were back, weary and happy and ready for a night's sleep. Keith called at seven the next morning. He had never doubted once. How could we fail with such warriors for God?

From then on the building went up as a miracle. My journal recorded the progress:

October 20 - Got permit signed for building the church today.

October 25 - Dug footings.

October 26 - Began building church today!

October 27 - Curley Cate, a disabled veteran and expert electrician, volunteered to do all the wiring free. He worked ten hours a day all winter. His only charge was to "keep my coffee cup filled."

October 27 - Today we had 108 in church, 48 in Sunday school, 25 in United Methodist Youth Fellowship. Appealed to people to buy blocks for one dollar each, used pews for sixty dollars each.

By the next Sunday the pews and blocks were all sold.

The next Saturday volunteers came to dig footings but we needed more workers to get ready to pour concrete when the volunteers from United Methodist Temple would come. Everything was done but finishing the hand digging. I prayed, then I headed toward the old tavern in Lacoochee.

I often stopped there when I was out calling, to witness to the men who lolled there in the sunlight, emptying their whiskey bottles. It was not the safest watering hole in Florida, but I knew the bartender, a bright young black man who had been my student at the college last semester. I told him I needed six men to dig footings for three hours.

"What will you pay?" he asked.

"Nothing. When they have needed food, clothes or medical help for their babies, Trilby Methodist Church has been there for them. When their kids have been in trouble, I've been in court with them. Now I am offering them an opportunity to do something significant that will last for eternity." By nightfall the footings were dug and new friendships cemented with these men who had taken seriously my ridiculous request. I had needed them, and they had proven that the church meant more to them than handouts.

October 31 - We had a Halloween carnival for needy kids held at the Moose Lodge to keep the children off the streets in this dangerous neighborhood on this dangerous night. More than four hundred kids enjoyed the spook house and ring throw, dart toss, dunking booth, bowling, kissing booth, cotton candy and pumpkin pie. All of it was free with donations going to UNICEF. We wanted those in need to be able to help others even more needy, so we put a huge picture of a starving African baby above the tin can offering box. The donations were amazingly generous, many from welfare checks.

November 11 - Vic Plessinger, a Mennonite contractor and volunteer, came up with the crazy idea of putting the main entrance at the side of the church, coming out of the old lean-to, instead of at the rear as in all "proper" churches. Some agreed, but it looked dead wrong to me. How can a bride come in at the side of the church? I invited him and some of the leaders home for supper so we could discuss it. Nothing was decided. I went to bed troubled. As is my custom, I wrote down twenty-five reasons why Plessinger might be right. It wasn't easy, but by morning I handed him my list. It began with: God has sent us a real contractor who has built churches before. There is no point in soliciting talent if we don't use it. We could remodel the old lean-to which connects the old and new churches into a foyer. If the kitchen were behind it, we could have an open window for serving coffee and fellowship in the foyer each morning. People would linger after church and get to know each other. The old mud hole in front of the lean-to could be made into a courtyard with a rose garden, fountain and inviting statuary and benches. This plan would perfectly fit the purpose of coming to church: Enter the prayer garden to pray and prepare your heart, enter the foyer to drink coffee and enjoy fellowship and enter the sanctuary to worship.

We put the door on the side. As it turned out, the building code required an exit door at the rear anyway. Here the bride comes in. The groom comes in at the side door. It is an absolutely perfect arrangement and the many weddings we have in our church affirm how God has a plan even when a church can't afford one.

Marilyn Wagster of Winter Gardens, a marvelous artist who

works in glass, heard of our work and offered to design, free of charge, exquisite floor-to-ceiling etched frosted chancel windows. She spent her entire August vacation designing them. We paid only the two hundred dollars for the glass for each window. In less time than it took to announce this miracle, families clamored to buy them as memorials. These designs are on file with the Pearcy Glass Company in Winter Haven, Florida, and we would be glad for other churches to use the patterns. Any small church can afford them and if one is broken they can be replaced with a mere phone call.

Enroute to pick up the windows, Jim and I saw an Italian stone artist skillfully plying his trade at a restaurant where we had breakfast. I marveled at the beauty of his work as he covered that building in stone, and I told him about our church. He was curious and dropped in the next Sunday, and the next and the next.

In a quiet moment, he shared his wounds. "I have built many churches for money but none for free. But I have had one *great* tragedy in my life. When I was young I was divorced and lost my little girl in that divorce. I told God I would put stone on your church for free, if he might see fit to let me find Frannie." I understood his bargain; I had done my own dickering at the market place of life. I prayed with him, and Jim and I pledged ourselves to be his prayer partners.

He kept coming to church, and soon he gave his heart to Christ. With no money on hand, I presented the idea of the stone to the church. I was sure the church would think it a luxury at a time when we needed so many other things, but I heard of a grant on Tuesday which was to be awarded on Thursday. Applications should have been made months in advance. I got a copy of the grant guidelines, wrote day and night, and on Thursday we had the money. The rock was important because we wanted a strong symbol of a permanent church. So many programs for the poor had come and gone.

Bright and early one morning, as I brought donuts and coffee to the workers, a gorgeous young Italian woman in cut-off shorts was helping our stone artist mix mortar. It was Frannie. She eventually yielded her life to Christ and started our singles group. The stone artist's new wife and his grandchildren also eventually accepted Christ. We were building much more than wood or stone. We were building the church triumphant against which the gates of hell could not prevail.

November 14 - We were expecting eighteen people to come on Saturday—tomorrow—from St. John's United Methodist Church in Winter Haven. Everything had to be ready for them. But the tree man didn't come to take down the tree. The plumber didn't show. The cement truck won't deliver on Saturday. The inspector didn't come. We would have to cancel the Winter Haven volunteers this Saturday.

It was three p.m. on Friday when Wilma Sapp, a saint of God in her sixties, called to ask what she could do.

"Get on the prayer line. Call everyone you know and ask them to pray," I suggested. By four o'clock the tree man was there. I called the cement man again and he said, "I don't know why I am doing this. I have to pay time and a half on Saturday, but we'll be there." The inspector called to say he had forgotten to come. He made a quick inspection and said he knew we would never try to do anything but perfect work, so we could go ahead. The plumber worked till midnight. For me, sleep would not come so I baked one of my famous pineapple upside down cakes, just to make sure we had a special treat when the crew arrived at seven o'clock the next morning.

November 17 - After the sermon, the congregation filed silently into the new church, and for the very first time in the new building, Keith and I offered the bread and wine. Tearfully, prayerfully, jubilantly, with the birds winging across that roofless sanctuary, we joined hands and sang the first hymn ever sung in that church: "Blest be the tie that binds our hearts in Christian love; the fellowship of kindred minds is like to that above."

November 19 - Jim and I celebrated our second anniversary. I had been afraid to take the church because I felt it might hurt our marriage, but it has done just the opposite. Every triumph, every trial has made us fall in love all over again.

Some time ago I had heard about an organization called Missionary Mobile Assistance Program (1736 N. Sierra Bonita Avenue, Pasadena, California 91104). Hundreds of their volunteers spend their retirement moving from church to church giving free building assistance. The only requirement for membership in MMAP is to be a "born again" Christian, own a mobile unit and be willing to work on at least four projects a year. The men build, do electrical and plumbing work and often, though not necessarily always, the wives help by sewing curtains, doing secretarial work, painting and even hammering nails. I sent an application to the MMAPers to help us build at Trilby.

In December the MMAP volunteers arrived. What a spiritual and material blessing they were! During the next five years, the sixteen MMAP teams that came and went gave us nine thousand free hours of expert construction help. They also taught Bible classes, sang in our choir and brought spiritual maturity to our church. We had taken in ninety new members and almost all were baby Christians who were eager to sit in Sunday school classes and learn rather than teach. Never once did the MMAPers mention their denominational backgrounds. When they worked with us they were as Methodist as Wesley.

Every time we needed a skill the new MMAP crew that came included just that talent. It made us certain that God was in charge of our building program.

Where there had been no United Methodist Women's organization for forty years, now the Trilby UMW was chartered, and every day it seemed they were doers of the impossible. Their pies and cakes kept the men working. They organized "Dinner Out" at the church. Each Sunday the church would buy the meat and the rest of us would bring the pot luck fixin's. They advertised, "If you are eating out Sunday, come eat with Trilby and help them build their church. Just 'tip' the Lord what it would cost you to eat out."

The Women's Bazaar was a huge success and provided money to finish building through December. The MMAPers went home to their own families. A new group of fourteen was due on January 5. Every cent we raised in December went to pay our apportionments in advance. We would close the year with them paid but not one cent in either building or general fund. Fourteen MMAP volunteers were due January 5. We needed three thousand dollars for Sheetrock by then.

December 6 - We went to the District Minister's Christmas party. The D.S. took me aside and said the conference had made a mistake in accepting my membership. He gave me a check for the pension I had paid thus far. I asked him who was responsible for the mistakes the conference made. The answer was "nobody." I was back to where I started in 1971 with the New Hope Church.

I asked to meet with the Board of Ministry at their December 21 meeting. I did and the minutes read, "I move that we accept the Missouri East Annual Conference records of the course of study and recognize Rose G. Sims' record of her years of service in that conference. We thereby recommend her as a local pastor in the Florida Annual Conference."

I told them I was not seeking to be a local pastor. I wanted the conference membership which I had been assured I had twelve years before when the bishop ordained me. They said I could meet again with the Board of Ministry and present my case. I met with them twice that spring. Both times they had none of my records before them. They asked ludicrous questions such as "Have you ever been to college?" and "Have you ever served in a church elsewhere?"

Throughout this ordeal, Jim was my staunchest supporter. With my ordination certificate and records in hand, Jim asked for a conference with Bishop Hunt. The bishop examined my ordination certificate and read the photo copied record of my ministry in the Missouri Clergy Journals.

"There is no question you had conference membership when you were ordained in 1973," he said. "You have been denied your appointment and pension benefits all these years. I will see that this comedy of errors is straightened out before I retire next year."

December 7 - Roland Strnad and other volunteers from St. John's of Winter Haven came to put on the roof. We also held our Christmas party for area children. The youth performed their musical, "Psalty's Christmas." This was their chance to share the gospel story and see that no child in Trilby and Lacoochee was without a gift. We sent invitations to the entire Lacoochee-Trilby Elementary School.

We were sure we had plenty of sacked oranges and candy but nearly five hundred children stormed our doors. There was no way we could get them all in the old church, so we presented two shows. I learned much later that one mother who was in labor waited outside in the cold for an hour for the second show. She said it was the only Christmas her children would get.

We did not have nearly enough candy or toys. The wives of the Winter Haven men had come along to help with the party. Inez Strnad got the word to the men on the roof. Five, ten and twenty dollar bills rained like manna from heaven. During the first show, the women raced to Dade City for more toys and candy.

After each show, each child was given a ticket for a new skirt or jeans. (The Day Star Catholic Mission across the street from my home in Dade City had given us eight hundred pairs of brand new designer jeans and skirts last October, which we had saved as a special Christmas present.) The church women were stationed at the parsonage-turned-mission, and each child was fitted and invited to the mission's monthly clothing give-away and to Sunday school and church.

The next day was the children's program at church. Arrayed in familiar looking jeans and skirts, they haltingly said their pieces to the applause of smiling parents. The youth did an encore of their musical and Santa arrived with treats for everyone.

Suddenly Santa walked over to the pastor to ask if she had been a good girl.

Had I? I wondered as Santa handed me a sack of candy and an orange. How glad I was that it was not my "goodness" that would buy my redemption. No, I had not always been good. I had resisted God's call, and I had often failed. There were still so many lost souls to be won. The ordination certificate signed by Bishop Goodrich was recognized by no one but myself. Maybe my real ordination had been the call to the altar of that little church when I was twelve years old.

Memories flooded my inner being as the years and the miles melted away. Once again I was a tiny depression-era waif in a snow-covered, one-room country church clutching the orange I had just been given. Bundled in scarfs and mittens, crunching the sparkling snow underfoot, I hugged it all the way home. It was the only orange I got all year, and I knew how to make it last, how to savor it down to the last bite of bitter rind. Oranges grew far, far across the world in a magic land called Florida where palm trees swayed and no one was ever poor, or cold or hungry.

Someday when I was rich and famous, I would go there and pick all the oranges I could eat. Then I would send one to every boy and girl in the world so no child would ever have to wait a whole year for this magic moment.

I wondered what the orange the migrant orange pickers' cherubs received this morning meant to them. I had seen these little ones out in the groves. The babies would be in baskets or strapped to a mother's back while the tiny first graders joined their brothers, sisters and parents in filling baskets hour after sweltering hour to make the day's quota enough to feed a family. Perhaps a juicy, crisp apple from faraway Washington's Wenatchee Valley would have brought the same magic I had known to these migrant children, but the oranges were free from Oakley Groves.

I longed to learn to speak in tongues—the tongues of the poor, the multi-ethnic, the apathetic, the teenage mothers, those without hope, the warehoused elderly, the lonely rich, the hungry and forgotten.

Soon the last hug had been given, the last "Merry Christmas" wished. We were invited out for dinner, but I asked Jim to go on ahead. I needed some time alone with God.

Christmas was over in the church. The parties, the concerts, the musical, the sermons, the giveaways, the caroling, the hundred things a country church does had been done.

Keith had turned off the heater before he left, and it was getting downright chilly in the church. The huge Christmas tree stood proudly but a bit tipsy, and the costumes and props so carefully created from castoffs now cluttered the chancel.

I was bone tired and starved. I had not eaten since the day before. There had been so many who needed Christmas baskets, and so much more that we couldn't pack into baskets. I had come home from calling long after midnight.

Suddenly I realized I was clutching my sack of candy and my orange as though I once again had to make Christmas last until springtime to drive away the snow and ice of poverty. I, who had a doctorate, who had been around the world, who could buy almost anything I wanted, was clutching that sack of candy. I hardly dared open it, wanting somehow to make Christmas last until the snow and ice of injustice, poverty, loneliness, drugs, crime, divorce and pain were gone.

Show me a sign, God, I prayed. I don't want to spend my life in a seemingly futile effort. I could not, like Scarlet O'Hara, end my life saying, "I'll think about that tomorrow."

"Miracle Worker, work one for me," I prayed.

And he did. God had not forgotten me. Cautiously, as in bygone days, I opened my Christmas bag of candy. There, just as I had done fifty long years ago, I found exactly the same red and green hard candy of my childhood. As a child I had never been able to figure out the miracle of how they had etched in gold, red and green hard candy the marvel of a tiny manger scene with the Baby Jesus asleep on the hay.

Tears flooded my soul as I savored the long forgotten minty sweetness, a magic gift from my childhood.

Suddenly I felt an overwhelming thankfulness to God for my pilgrim journey. I may have been widowed twice. I may not have my conference membership recognized. But who could ask more than the warmth and love of the Christmas spirit shared with these honest, saints and with Jim? They knew what Christmas was all about, and their contagious love had made it happen for the least, the lost and the lonely.

The country fried chicken and biscuits soon would be ready. My rendezvous was over. Enroute home I left my orange and candy with a tiny wheelchair-bound grandma living far from her children. She had become my mentor. The treat had done its healing for me; maybe it could be a second blessing to her.

11

The Quality of Niceness

All during Christmas Jim and I hunted in vain for Sheetrock. The manufacturer, Georgia Pacific, was on strike and we learned that there was not a sheet to be had in the entire Tampa area. Quite by accident (if God's plans are accidental) we met a man who had exactly the Sheetrock we needed stored in a garage. His church had planned to build with it until they had a "church split." Jim paid for it, and we went home to pack for a five-day vacation.

We picked up the mail and found a letter from St. John's Church in Winter Haven. "We always take a Christmas vesper offering," it read. "Usually we get about three hundred dollars. This Christmas we told the story of Trilby, of the children standing coatless, freezing for an hour in the courtyard, waiting for a simple doll or truck and sack of candy. We took an offering for your work." Enclosed was a check for $3,700. How gracious of God to lift the burden just in time for us to enjoy our little vacation.

The singles, now well organized, began "Thank God it's Friday" potluck suppers with tons of food, speakers and activities ranging from square dancing and clogging to musicals. Their fellowship soon became a major avenue for new members and leadership. The singles gave out hundreds of pounds of food every month and shared in counseling and evangelism. They named their group SASS.

Cal Duell, former president of SASS, claims that their two dollar spaghetti supper was the most expensive meal he has ever eaten. A building contractor, he joined the church, stayed to draw plans and signed his name and reputation to the youth center and education unit which was our next building project. He brought his beautiful girlfriend, Anita. One mellow September day Jim and I wended our way into the panoramic mountains of Tennessee. High on top of "God's Mountain," where Cal had years before helped build a retreat for youth, I made the bride's bouquet from wild mountain daisies and married them in the simple chapel that he had built.

We lost our singles president but gained a most faithful chairman of our building committee. Because so many of our singles eventually married and stayed in the church, there was never any line of division in fellowship between married and single folks. We all belonged to God's church.

I learned the local Parks and Recreation Commission had allocated funds for a program in all the affluent area cities, but not Lacoochee. My friends in the ministerial alliance and I got one thousand signatures protesting this injustice. The County Commissioners allocated nine thousand dollars; the next year it was increased to eleven thousand dollars. Now our youth find great summer employment and a chance to learn the names of so many more children and their needs and hopes.

February. The beautiful blue carpet for the church is here and pews installed. I suggested that the kitchen be eighteen by eighteen so it could double for Sunday school, adult education cooking classes and small meetings. The stove and refrigerator were recycled resources.

Never before had we had a stove, a dish, a pot or a pan. Word went out. Everyone took the surplus from their own kitchens and before the linoleum was laid, we mysteriously had exactly the pots and pans and utensils necessary.

April 12. We were not ready to move into the new church, but the old church could not hold the hundred and fifty who were coming. We took the one hundred-year-old cypress slat pews into the new church, brought in chairs and had our first worship service. Knowing that it was important to set the tone for worship, I preached on "Work for the night is coming, when man works no more." I said, "We justify our existence, not by adding years to our lives, but by adding life to our years. People grow old and discontented by deserting their ideals. Years may wrinkle your skin, but to give up interest wrinkles your soul. When your heart is covered with the snows of pessimism and the ice of discontent, then and only then are you old."

I concluded intensely, "Be afraid to die until you have scored some victory for God and your fellowman. You have indeed scored an internal victory but the battle has just begun." We ended by circling hands around the unfinished sanctuary as "Onward Christian Soldiers" rang from the rafters.

May 1. We installed the pews we had bought from the old Jupiter Tequesta Methodist Church for sixty dollars each. The Dunedin Church had donated their pulpit and communion table. The pews were beautiful but they seated only ninety and already we had chairs in every corner.

June 11. We dedicated the three-tiered, ornate steeple which Jim Early from the Ridge Manor Church had hand carved. The Fitzpatricks will be remembered for the steeple clock which turns the townfolks' attention God-ward as they pick up their mail. We bought a marvelous bell for forty dollars from an ancient bartender who sat with his six-pack in a dilapidated shanty. He had once owned a local watering hole. It had been his demise. I listened to his pain. I convinced him that God might be happy if the bell Satan once rang to entice people to sin might ring to call sinners to Christ. He agreed. I presented Christ, but he did not accept. I suggested our AA meeting, but he never came. I never pass that shanty but my heart goes homeward in compassion and love to all who struggle in pain.

For the first time in the ninety-year history of our church, we now had a real indoor toilet . . . two restrooms, both of them two-holers! The young people voted on who would be the first to flush it. Everyone else went outside and rang the bell in celebration.

We had a rousing Bible school and spent our vacation in Costa Rica, visiting Methodist missions. But the Devil works overtime in summer. I was also in court and prison with youth too young for the felony charges that cursed their futures.

Trilby again was first in the state in professions of faith-ratio and the conference sent me to Lake Junaluska, North Carolina, to receive the Circuit Rider Award. Each state "winner" had to tell their success story. A tiny, wiry, octogenarian whose suit hung on him like a scarecrow was the first speaker. When he finished telling how God had won in Georgia, I wanted the speeches to end and to give him all our awards. After the banquet I asked if he would come speak at Trilby. "Goodness no, lady," he replied. "You ain't got no idea of the lost people around me. I ain't had a day off in fifty years."

Our long range planning had included a youth center and education unit in the thirty by sixty foot lot behind our church. We were crowded to capacity, and the church unanimously voted to build again. Cal drew up fantastic plans for a two-story, poured concrete youth center and education building. The District Board approved it. Enthusiasm was never higher.

The district superintendent led the service at our third harvest festival. He offered to preach at the dedication and we set the date for January 18.

In describing the ways I've seen closed churches become revitalized, I have tried to include some constants. I now realize the only constant in the world today is CHANGE! What worked yesterday won't work today, so try something new. You never fail until you quit trying. What are young people thinking about, singing about, worried about? The many success stories in the most unlikely places ought to be taken more seriously than the dire predictions of experts who are not out there with their hands on the plow. We ought to be assimilating new insights and understandings of contemporary possibilities which may soon slip through our fingers.

We must stop touting, "Well, that happened because Bill was pastor." The question should be, "What is Bill doing that all of us could do?" The United Methodist Church, with its long history of decline, must not be threatened by excellence. It must demand it.

Once we let a new pastor in the pulpit, we should demand accountability. When I was a principal I asked to be invited into each room some time during the week when the teacher was succeeding. If she were failing, I took responsibility to find out where and to get her loving help. I hope I was not a threat. I had hired her and if she failed it showed my poor judgment. I had just as much at stake as she did.

Now I understand that principals are so burdened with paperwork that they have little time for people. It makes me wonder if the church is doing this to our D.S. and bishop?

I resisted to have a board meeting if there is nothing to discuss. Churches should get medals for lumping all their activities on one night so the people and the pastor can be home with their families on other nights. I avoid going to senseless meetings that are less important than my family. I want to be in church when they are and home when they are. God knows the world is beating down the walls of the family enough without the church's assistance.

We should recognize and encourage excellence. I used to tell my kindergarten class when they were all out of line, "I love the way Billy is in line." It works. In our church we give "Top Banana Awards."

It seems IBM had a new president who was smart enough to see that recognition often meant more than a salary raise. One day during a meeting a lowly employee came up with a brilliant idea. The president searched for an award but found nothing in his desk but his lunch. Quickly he pulled out his banana and said, "Congratulations, you have just been named Top Banana." That has now become the most prestigious honor in the company, one for which all the employees strive.

Jim knows the value of strip strokes. The Circuit Rider Award inspired the idea for a permanent trust fund to the Florida Conference. The interest from the capital investment will provide five hundred dollars each year to the pastor with the most professions of faith in churches under 250 members. It is called the Grindheim-Sims Award and will perpetually honor Oscar and Jim.

Trilby won it again this year, so we asked that it go to the next in line, Wol-Uk-Lee, a Korean pastor. He thanked us and said he would use it to start a building fund. The church uses Interbay Methodist Church for one o'clock Sunday afternoon services. But I told him the award was mad money for whatever luxury or fun time he and his family needed. Any pastor who wins that award has already given to the limit for the church. I remember Gaylie's joy at the twenty-five dollar funeral fee. I hope it serves a dual purpose, a well deserved pat on the back and a fun time with his precious wife and two darling little boys.

I wonder what would happen if we planned monthly or quarterly

Sunday afternoon area growth seminars for laity and clergy. These would not be held in stuffy conference rooms but in local churches—sometimes in upbeat growing churches, sometimes in churches where we could together see the need and respond with hands-on experiences. I am sure many churches would develop the kinds of "Partners in Missions" approach which built Trilby. I think it would make us all responsible for each other. New friendships would produce resources across church lines. I remember St. John's $3,700 Christmas gift in a time of desperate need. It came because they had an on-site experience. They saw the real live kids. Our churches are much too competitive and emotionally isolated.

The conference could also establish a seminary internship scholarship which must be served in a growing church. It would change the dismal image of the country church as a stepping stone and might curb the destructive, discouraging one and two-year pastorates. After a year in Trilby, a young pastor would picture a church such as ours as a cherished, treasured appointment instead of a jumping off place.

An eager, dedicated seminary intern would have been a godsend at Trilby. It would have freed me up for cherished time with my husband and children. It would give the intern rich insights no textbook can teach. In turn, the seminarian could share fresh ideas with a growing pastor.

We also need to stop stereotyping people. I once was asked to go to a Rural Life Center "to help recruit young men in our rural churches." Young men! What about old ladies? What about second career folks, retirees, persons with handicaps?

People often ask me, "May I ask how old you are, Rose?"

I always answer, "Yes," and leave it at that. I don't say that because it's none of their business, but because it encourages discrimination and discrimination labels competency. You are old when you have no more vision, ignore the youth and feel the good old days were better than tomorrow.

Two critical skills which need to be rewarded are skill in conflict management and criticism avoidance. New clergy fresh out of seminary who have not learned these two arts often start a pattern which they teach their people. It leads to nothing but frustration and burnout for them both. I believe it is a cancer which is eating our church.

I recently spoke in a magnificent church seating five hundred. The thirty-year-old pastor was in his fourth appointment, was washed up and worn out. He was well educated, handsome, enormously musically talented, a gifted speaker. His theology was biblical, his wife and children precious.

He was now leaving the ministry, old and bitter, his marriage breaking, his church in shambles. His criticism was directed to the church, the Board of Ministry, the bishop and district superintendent, his seminary, his wife, his people, other pastors, the world at large. His huge beautiful church was empty, his people bewildered and angry.

Bishop Hunt said, "All of us in ministry feel ill equipped for the avalanche of wounds we will have to heal . . . and the wounds we receive." Good conflict management and a pastor and people who have been taught criticism avoidance are ready to grow.

I recently called at the home of a youth member. The father proceeded to tell me that although he was raised a Methodist, he quit the United Methodist Church when they began ordaining "homosexuals and women."

"You lump us both together?" I laughed, while inwardly cringing. That laugh gave me an opportunity to share the forward steps the United Methodist Church has made this quadrennial in separating essential compassion for homosexual people from ordination to ministry. It also gave me a chance to model women clergy as caring, concerned, capable. He was in church last Sunday.

I can't say I am not human enough to try to fend myself against hurt. ("I don't mind being a doormat for God," the old saying goes, "but I'm not going to write WELCOME on it.") But every hurt usually indicates a hidden agenda of far deeper issues. I visited him again this week. We are becoming friends. His back-breaking burden is almost unbelievable. It has nothing to do with women ministers or others' lifestyles. I am so glad he has been introduced to Christ and a caring church.

Chips on the shoulder are like WET PAINT signs, begging to be challenged. Until we stop sweeping the hidden agenda in our dying churches under the rug and begin to find reasons to succeed rather than excuses to fail, we cannot begin to administer intensive care.

I once visited Vera, a precious eighty-year-old woman who was critically ill. Her grief-stricken husband told me the doctor had said,

"Phil, you can't expect your wife to live forever." That man immediately called a prayer meeting and changed doctors and remedies. Today his wife is home, I hope for years to come.

A church that works can be replicated, with modification, almost anywhere. Every person's needs are identical . . . love, ego, friends, faith and so on. Until we learn that, we will make the mistake of saying, "It may work in a little country church, but how about a big rural or city church that is closing? It may work while a man is pastor, but what if we have a woman or a black?" But it can happen in every conceivable community. We are all building the same church.

Trilby is a church in a town of less than a hundred people with at least seventeen churches in a three mile radius. Many are dilapidated, store front or "spite" churches salvaged out of two or three "church splits." We don't lack for churches in this area.

Why, then, did Trilby United Methodist Church take off? Perhaps our growth happened because we built the nicest church, performed the nicest outreach and enlisted the nicest people who say the nicest things. We learned simple, hard work shows our commitment to a very nice God who suffered and died for all of us so prone to not be nice.

That sounds like a corny, naive evaluation. But, who can question the quality of just plain niceness? I have married three very nice men. I have tried to be nice to them. It has been very nice. Being a pastor has been nice. Jim thinks being a clergy spouse is nice. Niceness is sometimes fun, sometimes hard work, always attainable.

I never did like garbage cans. They are not nice. Great, gray, greasy, groaning things with gaping mouths, they are always ready to fill their innards with the refuse carelessly cast off by humanity.

I especially don't like garbage cans at front doors of churches.

It wasn't really the front door. It was the back door, but the easiest place to park at the Hallsville Church was in the back lot. So the back door was the logical place to enter.

The rusty garbage can had stood there for years. Early each Sunday morning as I passed the Hallsville Church with its garbage can enroute to my first preaching assignment at Red Rock ten miles away, I would stop, pick up the garbage can and hide it along the side of the church.

But when I got back to Hallsville just in time for the eleven o'clock morning service, the garbage can would invariably be back in its old spot. The dear saint who "tended to the church" had been there early, done a little "sweepin' up" and put it back where "it belonged."

It bothered me to think that that garbage can might symbolize the life of the church. So much garbage, so many hurts, had almost closed the church. Little wounded feelings, untended, unlistened to, pile up in the life of a church. Finally the church decides to call it quits and there is a handy garbage can of neglect to throw them all into.

But now the Hallsville Church was waking like some sleeping giant, stretching its limbs God-ward, flinging aside the garbage of the past and burying it deep in the sea of God's forgetfulness.

Then, why the garbage can? These were my thoughts as I was returning from a "country burying" with a twenty-five dollar honorarium tucked in my clerical robe.

Tooling along Highway 61, brilliant scarlet caught my eye. Blazing geraniums, millions more than I had seen before, glorified the roadside vegetable market. Red is such wonderful color. After death and pain, I had gotten a red car, a red coat and had planted the parsonage with red geraniums. Why make life more dreary with black? Why not flaunt the brilliant red of hope?

And why not? Why couldn't a mountain of red geraniums replace the garbage can? Funeral fee in hand, robe shed, I began selecting the choicest pregnant three-bloomers, sturdy and defiant of winter storm or church traditions. I stopped by a dairy farm for gunny sacks of cow manure and a shovel. Dream in hand, the farmer decided to accompany me. We finished late that night. Wearily, I turned in, anticipating the morning when I would not have to remove the garbage can. It was safely tucked around the side of the church, a mountain of gorgeous geraniums planted in its stead.

Nobody said a word about my geraniums at the morning service. But a week later, I noticed that new geraniums had sprouted all around the church. Like a halo of gleaming red, they encircled the street side of the church.

Every Sunday we had a children's story for the many neighborhood kids who were now filling our church. I would gather them all up front, sit down on the steps of the altar with them to minimize the discrepancy of our sizes and give them a thought for a growing week.

One special week, I had instructed Matt to bring in the old garbage can. What a howl of laughter as everyone remembered how the garbage king had been dethroned.

"Life's like that," I told the kids. "You get a lot of garbage in your life: sins you would rather throw away, thoughts you can't live with, hates you should never have harbored. You throw them in the garbage can, but they keep showing up again and again. Same old can, same old place. To make it disappear you have to plant something beautiful in its place, like love, hope, courage, kindness and truth."

Octavia, Nebraska, where Oscar served in the 1950s, had exactly one hundred people. The Brethren and Baptist churches federated. There had been rivalry between those two churches until, gasping for breath, they shook hands and joined forces.

After an extensive building program and five years, we saw formerly opponent families inviting each other over for Sunday dinners. "It can happen anywhere and must happen everywhere" is not a fantasy limited by the size of the church, the town, the circumstances or the problem.

Tragically, our seminaries, pastors, district superintendents and bishops are not required to take courses in conflict *prevention.* We always talk about conflict management instead. We will always spend our days majoring in minors if we devote our time to battling the saints rather than settling the sin question. That is why Jesus came to save us and that is the example his life taught.

March came and we cancelled the last MMAP project because we could not get our building permit without more parking space. I am alarmed that Methodists are selling land and churches. The population is growing and nobody will make more land. There was just no land available near the Trilby Church, no old house we could tear down, no nearby vacant lot. We longed for an acre or two or for someone smart enough to figure out a parking plan that would pass the commissioners.

I earnestly feel we should be hoarding the land of our forefathers, and buying more of it. Instead, we are selling it for a pittance because we lack the foresight of our fathers. If only someone had done that we would easily have had our permit. Dying churches are not blessed with foresight.

In addition to the parking problem, we faced a second hurdle. The Historical Society was unhappy that we would have to remove the octagon-shaped addition which had been tacked on to the one hundred-year-old church chancel decades ago. They had put a historical marker on the church and resisted the change. It was a little alcove with two windows providing a cross breeze for the pioneer preacher.

But we needed that space for a double door to join the old church and make a larger social hall and Sunday school area.

We had spent the winter remodeling the old church, rewiring the ancient electrical system, replacing the termite-ridden floor and painting inside and out. It was now ready to serve in a hundred ways as space we so desperately needed.

The old church, like a venerable saint, was feeble. We could have torn it down and solved our parking problem, but we sensed the importance of listening to the Historical Society and to the one or two for whom this was a sacred altar. We will keep it in repair as long as we can. It truly is a beautiful, spiritual antique and provides a warm welcome to the many who come from far and near with memories of a childhood church no longer standing. If the old church could talk, I think it would tell us it is delighted to be a silent witness to the score of activities it houses . . . UMYF, indoor volleyball, Scouts, wheelchair dancing, Sunday school, children's church and on and on.

Our latest and probably most successful use of the old church is Friday night country, western, gospel nights. We replaced the termite-ridden floor with new wooden boards, and the finest musicians from far and wide came to rehearse on Friday nights. Music lovers came to listen, tap their toes or sing along. After a bounteous covered dish dinner which mixes church folks with strangers, the tables are rolled up and the fiddles, guitars, and banjos make the sweetest music this side of the Mason-Dixon line. The sanctuary is left open, lights are on and many who never attend church wander in, feel at home and come back on Sunday. We call it "the alternative to the bar scene." Without spending a cent, singles, married, young and old mix and enjoy a church "date" night. After St. John's gave us a pool table, fooz ball and ping pong we gutted the old mission and opened it up for youth. With the nursery next door it truly becomes family night at the country church. Why shouldn't the church provide the best in social life to united families?

We do not feel we have desecrated it by outgrowing it as a sanctuary. Would it be more pleased if we had left it closed, unpainted, falling down and silently agreeing that "God is dead"? Our church is full of folks, including the pastor, who are not quite as good as new but not ready for the trash heap either.

Patience with purpose is productive. I knew we would build. We just had to figure out a way. God had sent the people. Surely he would send the space. The winter folks were going home. We had enough room for right now and there were other battles to win. My own deep personal need was for disciplined growth in his Word. The church bought dozens of volumes of *Through the Bible in a Year,* and we lined them up on the altar rail. Anyone could take one if he would promise to read it through. We suggested a price and left an offering plate. Young and old hungrily snatched them up. We had to order and reorder.

I was amazed at those who quietly told me they were reading the Bible through. They included a young single man who worked in corrections, a tough old man who never smiled, a sexually abused child we had rescued and our teenagers. I found enormous strength and new sermon material in this discipline. Jim and I grew strangely spiritually bonded as we shared our reading.

A pastor who neglects his spiritual life and sermon preparation does not need to wonder why he preaches to empty pews. We have, at best, only twenty-six hours of Sunday morning preaching time a year—so we cannot afford to waste a moment.

12

Building Bridges at Eventide

Through the grapevine I heard that St. John's United Methodist Church in Sebring was building anew and had some "New England" solid oak furnishings. Jim and I headed south to check this out. I was utterly amazed at the quality of this ostentatious find. I had prayed that God's house in Trilby would be the most sacredly beautiful spot in that sin-soiled city, but I had never dared to dream of such resplendent beauty. I was certain the price would overwhelm us. That's when I learned about recycled resources. The St. John's Methodist Church in Winter Haven had lovingly given them to the Sebring Church when they had outgrown them. Now Sebring gladly and freely gave us the gigantic gift worth thousands of dollars. For good measure, they threw in the intricately designed chancel vestments in brilliant green, purple, red and white for each liturgical season.

Now Trilby could also know the joy of being a giver. Our blue pews seating ninety became a miracle to another small, struggling church. Their verbose, tearful gratitude warmed our hearts. We had

had our share of miracles. Now we were thrilled to make them happen for another church.

Every place we had put our foot was claimed. No building in this entire impoverished area could compare in beauty, splendor and sacred loveliness. I spent the night in prayer and thanksgiving and a day in fasting for joy.

The January MMAP volunteers included a wood craftsman who ingeniously used the many assorted pieces of railing to transform our chancel into a masterpiece.

Jim had insisted that the architect's plans be revised to widen the church three feet and lengthen it thirty. The pews fit like a glove and seated 250. God had those pews in mind for us long before we knew there was a church in Sebring.

When January 18 arrived the church was packed for the dedication with dignitaries, ministers and laity from area churches. The district superintendent was listed on the front bulletin cover as the main speaker. The churches that had helped us to build came. Our choir sang. A Catholic priest, Father Paul, was there with his guitar choir.

The music was over. No district superintendent. It had come time for the sermon. With a prayer in my heart, I began.

Before me sat God's choicest saints whose toil, tears, dollars and devotion had raised this magnificent temple. Tomorrow would bring new battles, but for today the victory was won.

Three years of birth pangs for this country church. Now with the cries of a new baby, and labor pains all forgotten, God had again come down from heaven at Christmas with a baby in his arms. The church had indeed been born in spirit and in mortar.

Fresh as a gift from God, we had dressed her up. I painted verbal pictures of all the stalwart, saintly men and women whose prayer and love had guided our pilgrimage of faith. I challenged them to make it their call. Let us not call our task complete until America sees that it can and must happen everywhere.

Here, right before them, was the answer Wesley would have applauded. Here were the people who had done it. I thought of the hundreds and hundreds of people in dying churches who only need proof that it can happen. All of us must be leaders, pioneers and risk takers to make it happen anywhere and everywhere.

The next Wednesday I was scheduled for my annual appointment visit with the district superintendent.

He told me he had driven right by Trilby on Sunday on his way home, but he had just forgotten. He is a good man, a dedicated Christian. I know it was not intentional. When we learn that "all things work together for good," we will stop wasting time on needless judgment. Actually, although I would have been proud to have him speak, in my heart of hearts, as we built and labored I had cherished the thought of being the one to dedicate the new church. That intense yearning had been a dream only God and I shared.

The dedication had gone well. God's Spirit had been present, full of love and power. So it was with joy and optimism that I had come to this conference with the D.S.

"There are many conference members who, knowing you are not a member of the conference, feel it is unfair that you are serving a better church than they are. Should you leave tomorrow I would have no trouble replacing you."

It was not meant to be an insensitive remark, and it was not typical of this fine D.S. I tried to excuse him. Maybe it had been a rough day.

When the conference was ended, there had been no word of commendation, no thanks for apportionments paid in advance, a debt-free building, or leading the state in professions of faith. I rose to my feet, gave him a hug and turned my heart homeward.

It did not help that when I got home there was a letter with a denial to meet with the Board of Ministry this year to discuss conference membership. I had served four full years in Missouri and been denied, and the BOM minutes said they had accepted this. The BOM indicated that they had decided to call my first two years at Trilby supply. I would need to do six years in all to qualify.

Something had to be done, not for me, as I would be retiring soon, but for others who are less financially secure who would follow me. A young person with a growing family to support could not afford to be denied important job benefits to which he or she is entitled year after year. As we shared our devotions, Jim picked 1 Corinthians 13. He read, "If you love someone you will be loyal to him no matter what the cost. You will always believe in him, always expect the best of him, and always stand your ground in defending him" (author's paraphrase). Jim called the bishop, who saw us gladly. Jim made certain the Board of Ministry file was brought before him.

Bishop Hunt examined my transcripts. "You really do have an earned doctorate." What had he been told? Is that why the conference had treated me as an impostor?

The ordination certificate which had hung on my wall for fifteen long years was now in the bishop's hand. He said, "Did Bishop Goodrich ask you the ordination questions and lay hands on your head?" He knew the answer. I had the journal records affirming my ordination.

He researched every loophole. I could not have been ordained a local deacon in 1973, because local deacons were discontinued in 1968. "Even if they cancel two of your years in Florida, with the new ruling that two half years count as a whole, you have twelve full years. Nothing in Discipline 419 says it has to be done in one conference."

My ordination certificate in hand, he declared, "There is absolutely no question in my mind that you have had conference membership since 1973 and we have denied you every right ordination affords . . . appointment, tenure, pensions, insurance, promotion."

"The Board of Ministries is meeting all week. Can we settle it now?" I asked.

"Wait until next year. I promise I will have it for you before I leave office. This is not a matter of just Rose Sims, this is clearly a matter of justice and right."

Bishop Hunt had used the words justice and right! Suddenly I saw that I was not all alone. I was surrounded by a vast host of faithful reapers in lonely outposts of God's harvest field whose enviable record I could never match. I had silently, with great helplessness, listened to their horror stories. Many had simply left the ministry, quietly fading into the woodwork. Others traded their call for a divorce. Then powerless, with no tenure, they were left homeless and abandoned, stripped of everything except their call.

The meeting was over. Jim and I left the bishop's office and went to a huge downtown church where I had been asked to conduct a church growth seminar. With all their endowments, including a spacious gym and high-rise towers for the elderly, they were losing members and had fewer attending worship services than Trilby. I wished my project kids could have a gym like that. There would be room for a day care center so the children of Trilby's migrants would be safe. (One tiny Hispanic had his arm cut off in a tomato sorter the week before.) And I would appoint every lonely senior citizen boxed into that high rise honorary grandma or grandpa to a child who had none.

Annual Conference was coming. This would be my fourth appointment to Trilby, making four full years served. I was eligible for conference membership on those grounds alone. Then I remembered Hallsville and Red Rock. I searched in my mind for any reason that could be invented to deny me conference membership this time. I was battle scarred and exhausted. Maybe I should retire, I thought.

All around me stretched a grown up version of the mystical Florida of my childhood dreams. Palm trees swayed on endless white sand beaches. Retirees romantically danced the night away under the mellow tropical moon, played endless games of shuffleboard, golfed on manicured courses, slept late every morning, took cruises to exotic ports and dined out by candlelight at chic watering holes from Pensacola to Palm Beach.

From autumn until spring, they packed the churches and overflowed the parking lots. Many a faithful saint, worn out by the struggle of the dying American churches, sat back and for once let somebody else worry. "It looks tempting," I said to Jim.

I had promised I would retire if he would. He said he would if I did. He was an outstanding success as a media specialist and at the top of the pay scale. His bright, wonderful love for people made his work seem like play.

But I decided to stay. I remembered the churches I had had to leave before their roots were grounded. Too many later pastors had used them as springboards. Immature plants cannot be uprooted without damaging their tender roots. I reread the poem about the old bridge builder.

> He crossed the chasm deep and wide,
> Then turned back and built his bridge at eventide
> "You never again will pass this way,
> Why build you a bridge at the close of day?"

Although retirement never looked so good and I sometimes felt I had built enough bridges, the temptation faded when I looked at Trilby. Youth hung around the church day and night. For many it was the only safe harbor in a world of crisis. To them, the church provided parents and grandparents, faith and love. We were building our bridges at eventide . . . for them.

Once when a church Oscar served became part of a circuit, the new pastor commented, "It will be a snap. All I have to do for the extra four thousand dollar a year is preach my same old sermon one more time. Not bad money for an hour's work." The church had died. Every church is fragile, new ones tragically breakable.

I still had a thousand dreams yet to come true for Trilby. I had to find a Methodist Hispanic helper. The migrants needed daycare. The Health Department said they would take out liability insurance if we could get a retired doctor to open our clinic two days a week. We needed a playground for the kids; the Parks and Recreation Department suggested we use their land adjacent to the church on an "Adopt a Park" program. We would keep it fixed up; they would own it. That would provide a place for Little League, scouting and a recreation area for the neighborhood. We now had experienced Children's Church and Sunday school teachers. The singles were distributing hundreds of pounds of food, and the women kept the community's needy in free clothes. This fall five people would go to Evangelism Explosion training.

The tender shoots had blossomed and grown heavy with golden fruit. Why leave when it was just ready to pick? What could I ever do in retirement that would be half as much fun, allow me to make half as many real friends or give me half as much satisfaction as serving Trilby?

13

A Palm Sunday to Remember

The miracles at Trilby never ceased. Cal Duell was a contractor who knew about permits. Allen Cole's trailer park was new and shaky when I challenged him to give free space to the MMAPers. His Seven Acre Park was now packed, and he was building again, but not before he also had learned a lot about permits. We had gained the respect of the good people of the Building Commission, paying our dues to them and to the Historical Society. We had been bridge builders. There is no price tag on good will, but without it you can close your church doors.

Trilby UMC's bright, "know how" professionals drew up a new building plan, and this time it was accepted. We had our permit for the new educational unit. No sooner said than done, footings were in and walls were going up.

We had our first Cub Scout troop, and Boy and Girl Scouts followed. Suddenly I no longer felt tired, discouraged or defeated. I could hardly wait from Sunday to Sunday.

Our theatre group presented *The Music Man* with a cast of forty to a standing room only audience.

As our magnificent chancel became River City, USA, I wondered if it would be possible to keep the love and unity while we did a secular musical at the sacred altar. Nevertheless, there was a magical glow about those days of rehearsal. And we were keeping the kids off the street.

Michael Gunn, a gifted third grade teacher who co-directed the musical, accepted Christ during *The Music Man*. He later became one of our best Evangelism Explosion teachers. He was the 139th member to be received at Trilby during the first three years. Almost all came on profession of faith.

Henry Opperman, a retired United Methodist minister, shared a unique ministry with us which he called Knucklepower. We filled one thousand gift packages with candy, pencils, a Gospel of John, a tract or two and a list of all area churches and the time of their services. On the reverse side was a letter about our church, welcoming everyone to our open doors . . . children, youth, seniors and singles, Scouts, AA, the clinic, counseling, etc.

Twenty-seven of our lay people visited hundreds of homes. We went out in teams of three. One person drove while the other two knocked on doors. "Hello! We're calling from Trilby United Methodist Church. We would like to give you a little gift. We hope you will attend the church of your choice." The driver made notes about tricycles, bikes or children in the yards, and we made a special point to follow up. That job is never finished.

The youth had their own Knucklepower program. After an all-night lock-in, during which they cleaned the church spic and span, fifty youth enthusiastically called on five hundred homes. In a high crime area where people are afraid to open their doors, it was quite a sight to see the neighborhood invaded by wholesome, excited teenagers sharing their exuberant faith.

Fall came, and we had building to do. The MMAPers came back as the wild geese flew overhead. Our majestic sanctuary was now the site of many weddings.

Life comes full circle. At last I could laugh at having been married three times. I still had all three wedding dresses and they, and a closetful of formals I had also accumulated, were loaned out time and again. Couples would call and say, "We just want to get married." Nobody "*just* wants to get married." I tell them, "A wedding is for a day, but a marriage is for a lifetime. Still, for that day, let's make it a memory you can hold in your heart through sunshine and shadow."

I found a marvelous marriage questionnaire which I ask engaged couples to fill out. It pinpoints areas they have covered in private and those they want to discuss with me. Religion is often the one thing they haven't discussed. Many a bride and groom accepted Christ while preparing to accept each other. Our young adult class was growing.

Weddings were a happy relief from the many grim duties of the ministry, and Jim and I threw ourselves into the excitement. Many times I played the organ, baked the cake and decorated the church. Jim, being a photographer, often shot a couple of rolls of film and gave them to people who otherwise wouldn't have a single photo of their red-letter day. Sometimes I sent the couple off with a night's lodging away from "his" and "her" kids.

Through the years I buried children and grandmothers, suicides and murders, those who died of drugs and alcohol, heartbreak and old age, or just plain loneliness.

My counseling load was endless, and Jim's love of people was also sought for many a confidence. He found a doctor and insulin for a teenage diabetic. Youth often said, "I wish you were my dad." He was a good role model.

When I begged to know what I could get him for Christmas, his only request was to take the most needy kids out for dinner. After huge pizza supremes, he gave each of them money for a shopping trip. Two hours later they returned with gifts for their family, but not a single thing for themselves.

I visited jails, bail-bond offices, court, emergency rooms. We temporarily housed a teenager whose stepfather had tried to kill him. We found homes for runaways and throwaways, kids who had been kicked out of their homes.

Our story was written up as the "Church Aflame," a sort of national "Church of the Month" award which appears in a United Methodist newspaper. Each month's story features one growing church and tells the "why" of their growth so others can share their ideas. The response was overwhelming. Churches have had too much bad press; people were hungry for good news.

Evangelists Chuck and Fran Phelps saw the enormous need in our area and spent the entire winter. Each afternoon, with paints, a huge easel and some youth in tow, they headed for the housing projects. Like the Pied Piper of old, this simple farmer turned evangelist brought bus load after bus load of kids to church and to the Lord. The adults awaited his illustrated story each Sunday morning as eagerly as the children.

Chuck introduced us to Willie Watts and the Light Company, and we held a one-week Children's Revival. Our youth operated the more than 150. More than two hundred youngsters sat on the edge of their seats each night and many answered the altar call. They swelled the roll of our Sunday school and made the need for our new building acute. Classes had spread to the church lawn and winter was coming.

Fortunately, by now the walls were going up. This time Keith Pire was not alone. I remembered our rainbow under the old pecan tree. Since the very beginning, he had been the "go-fer." He wore out a pickup and drove thousands of miles for God. He was past seventy, often in pain, and his wife was in chemotherapy. But he never said no. I was glad this time he had helpers—plumber Richard Shere and his son and contractor Cal Duell.

This building would boost the replacement value of our property to nearly four hundred thousand dollars. If I had mentioned this three years ago, nobody would have believed me. Now, nobody said a word. Nothing was impossible with God. The MMAP crew came and there was always just enough material for each month's building.

In October I received word that I had been awarded the Circuit Rider Award, one thousand dollars and a trip to Atlanta to receive the award. Once again, America was seeing it could happen anywhere and must happen everywhere.

The harvest moon was still in the sky on one bright October Saturday when I headed for the church to put on the coffee pot for the volunteers. I hadn't been able to sleep. I thought about the countless women and men who had not won an award.

Trilby's streets were deserted and its houses dark as the morning sun cast its golden rays on the steeple clock. It was the top o' the morning . . . five o'clock. Somewhere a rooster announced the dawn with a muffled crow. In the courtyard, a memorial to my mother from my loving sisters, the diamond dewdrops sparkled on every rose petal. The flag waved lustily in the cool morning breeze, proclaiming, "liberty and justice for all."

Slipping off my shoes, tears of joy blinding my eyes, I retraced my steps of three Octobers ago. The briars were gone.

Left! Right! Press on! Praise God! March on! The trumpets of God were blowing. Not one of his words had failed. Here on this empty lot God had built a sanctuary, here a mission, here an education building, here a youth center.

I was back where I began. I unlocked the door and quietly slipped into the sanctuary. The sun was bursting through Ruth Sims' memorial window with its gentle shepherd cradling the newborn lamb. A beam of crimson sunlight shone on the pew which Sunday had been filled with black, Hispanic and Anglo children. Another fell on the pulpit, dedicated to Oscar, where I spoke God's Word Sunday by Sunday. I fell to my knees in wonder at God's loving kindness to me.

That wonderful newness of his presence which I had felt on my last farewell to Oscar encompassed me. I thought, "Oscar, can you hear me? As you won the Rosa O. Hall Award, I have won the Circuit Rider Award. For this final and last time, before my life is over, we can affirm loud and clear nationally that 'it can happen anywhere and it must happen everywhere.'"

The echo came back, "Not until there is justice and vision and evangelicals in the pulpit can it happen anywhere and everywhere."

It was time again for my annual appointment conference with the district superintendent. This time Jim went with me and the bishop had asked to see us afterwards. In front of the D.S., Bishop Hunt assured me, "You have had conference membership since 1973 and have been denied all rights, but you will have it this year." He asked me to prepare a folder documenting my long struggle for recognition as an ordained Methodist minister. He again used those words I hardly dared to let myself use . . ." It is a matter of justice and right."

Unless I could get conference membership, which assures appointment, salary, pension and benefits, how would evangelicals follow in my footsteps? Our model would be lost eternally. Bishop Wilke had sounded the alarm loud and clear: We are an endangered species which is near extinction. But of all people, I had seen the miracles that made such a pronouncement ludicrous.

Jim prepared the notebook and I sent a copy to the Board of Ministry and the bishop. I asked to meet with the Board, but the notebook was promptly returned with a letter stating, "You cannot be seen until your four years are completed. Your first two years were merely supply. You are now in your second year. Come and see us in two years."

Back home at Trilby, Evangelism Explosion fires were burning brightly. The five I had requested from God who had gone to Ft. Lauderdale to take training in Evangelism Explosion were a Pentecost in our midst. Like the new believers in Acts, "Everyone was filled with awe."

The church served an elegant Evangelism Explosion banquet for our prayer partners, trainers and trainees to launch the sixteen weeks of training. Every Thursday, teams combed the area calling on rich and poor, parishioners and prospects. Pentecostal fires burned. These people were speaking in tongues . . . the understandable tongues of evangelism . . . loud and clear! People heard in their own language the Word of God. Many of the poor, the rich, the lost and the lonely now understood clearly enough to accept Jesus Christ as their personal Lord and Savior. Spring was here. Snowbirds with Michigan and Ontario license plates were clogging the highways, headed north where snow was melting and grandchildren were anxiously waiting. I longed for springtime in Missouri with the redbuds and dogwood in bloom and especially for my own precious grandchildren.

The last MMAP crew was finishing the youth center. The air conditioning was in and the walls were painted a soft rose with a companion wallpaper in delicate roses. The heavy satin drapes were hung. Money was given for a fireplace. The bathrooms were gorgeously papered and furnished.

We sang "Something Beautiful, Something Good." It was more beautiful than I had ever dared dream it could be on that October day so long ago. The children and youth who came needed a pattern to aspire to . . . a beautiful model. The AA needed a place of dignity and worth. It was a luxury. A check came in the mail from Iowa. The accompanying note simply said, "Get what you need for the church." Jim doubled the check. He knew how much it meant to the kids.

A United Methodist Women's committee gleefully went shopping and came home with elegant velvet lounges. Elise donated a dozen comfortable individual matching chairs. The picture of Christ which had hung in the old church was reverently placed above the mantle. An elegant dining table for teas and wedding receptions along with floor lamps made the room cozy and inviting. No interior decorator could have furnished the room more tastefully than those talented UMW women.

Money to pay as we went had been hard to come by. There had been no more grants. We were no longer a novelty but had become a respectable church. But God hadn't forgotten us. Now there were new people who surprised us with their generosity. This time when we were desperate for Sheetrock, an attorney who left the United Methodist Church but had grown up with great Wesleyan revivals and altar calls slipped three thousand dollars into the Sunday offering plate.

We "sold" the six rooms upstairs for seven hundred dollars each with a promise that the donor's name would be memorialized with a plaque on the door. I simply appealed for the hundredth time, "I would like to give you the opportunity to do something significant that will last for an eternity." The rooms were quickly oversold. Love ever gives, forgives, outlives and ever stands with open hands. Those retirees whose names will for posterity be engraved on the doors in this poverty-stricken community had done themselves a favor and they knew it.

We needed a breather. The winter people were gone and we could get along without the rooms until fall. The huge upstairs was complete except for partitions and finishing. The curtains were already made and the wallpaper bought at a closeout sale. The nursery would be yellow, pink and blue. The toddlers' room would have circus elephants, and bright red curtains.

I suggested installing chandeliers in the new downstairs parlor. We needed the atmosphere that would be provided by crystal chandeliers with a dimmer switch for elegant dinners for singles, intense group sessions for youth, just fun times and coffee hours or UMW meetings.

But the men could not see it. I did not press the issue. Their vision had been stretched to capacity. The gigantic two-story concrete cast building Cal had risked his license to engineer had been his dream and it had far exceeded my vision. The men had faithfully, though not always having the same opinion, completed the building with honest admiration and love for each other. Because we had begun our building program with the idea that only God can judge, not a single step in the entire three-year building program was marred by conflict or confrontation. How can we expect families and nations to avoid war unless the church models peace and unity?

The men did not see the necessity for the chandeliers the women had envisioned but had conceded for carpeting and Sheetrock instead of the linoleum and bare block walls they had thought were all we could afford. Nobody wins a war. Everyone wins peace. Christian fellowship is the relationship of men and women who, by the power of the Holy Spirit, participate in the life and work of Christ.

The morning the room was complete, the book of Acts came alive. Everyone was in awe and wonder at beauty beyond their wildest dreams. When the invitation was given, seven knelt at the altar. Each was accompanied by a disciple who had shared Evangelism Explosion and asked the final question: "Does that make sense to you?"

The Christian Television Network asked me to do three one-hour satellite interviews beamed to millions. The response was overwhelming. The pain experienced by those sitting at the deathbed of their beloved churches broke my heart.

Ringing in my ears were the horror stories of Board of Ministry rejections I had heard in greatest confidence over many years. Speech majors were given contingencies of speech courses. Those who succeeded were told to come back when they were humble. Evangelicals were told they read the Bible too much. Women were too emotional or not emotional enough. Too bossy or too timid. Others were too fat, too old, too proud, too lazy, too intense. Married clergy couples faced moves to opposite ends of the state. Nonclergy spouses at the peak of their careers were forced to choose between unemployment or separate households. Men and women with Wesleyan zeal and results were often locked out of the ministry. Small wonder the clergy trail was strewn with shattered marriages, destroyed egos, breakdowns, breakups and burnout. The United Methodist *Discipline* does not give the Board of Ministry unbridled power, yet that group controls the very theology of the church by its ability to determine who can and cannot speak from Methodism's pulpits.

Only Jim's enormous commitment to Christ and his love for me had enabled me to weather Trilby. He worked Monday through

Friday. I was busiest on Saturday, the only day volunteer crews from other churches could help, and Sunday. No week has eight days.

The Trilby people are most accommodating. Jim planted himself, and they cushioned our marriage with deep respect. The administrative board understood Jim was a top priority. The success of their church could only be enhanced by my success in marriage.

Jim's spring break came. Chuck, who with his saintly wife, Fran, had braved the winter cold in the drug-ridden Lacoochee projects day after day with his easel and his winning, magnetic witness, would soon be leaving us. He promised to lead the Palm Sunday service for me.

The open road was calling. Jim and I left Friday after school, two happy wanderers with seven whole days to spend in utter abandon. I wanted to see Florida, not the tourist Florida, but the haunts of the creative retirees. The MMAP workers had described the many projects they had built all over the state. We saw the Bradenton Missionary Village where houses are provided rent free to retired missionaries. I now understood why I have never seen an unhappy MMAPer. Often feeble in strength or plagued by illnesses, they labor to build God's kingdom.

We saw youth camps and Teen Missions and Biblia. We journeyed across the Seminole Reservation and talked with a creative Native American pastor whose work far excelled mine. Jim left funds to educate a pastor in Zaire. We enlisted a team of ten Teen Mission youth from eight nations to conduct a weekend revival for our youth in December.

This Palm Sunday I would be a layperson and sit in the pew as I had not done for many years. I needed to be fed, to have someone else pronounce God's benediction. I wanted to visit a Haitian minister friend's church and honor him with a donation.

But Jim insisted he wanted to hear Chuck preach in Trilby. It made no sense to me. I loved Trilby, but I needed this break.

Nevertheless, I conceded to Jim because it seemed important to him, and he is important to me. Palm Sunday found us at Trilby just in time for Jim to slip into his choir robe. The parking lot and every street north, south, east and west was jammed.

We parked behind the mission. Every pew was full and chairs were set in the aisles. Someone got up and gave me his seat.

I had never been a "parishioner" in this church. I thought, if I were a stranger looking for a church home, here is where I would plant my roots, without a moment's hesitation.

The air was pungent with the sweet, sweet spirit of love. The singing was spirited and genuine, and joyful hugs were exchanged across lines of color, age and gender. The church looked magnificent from back here. I had never seen this view. Eight huge trailing ferns brought the outdoors inside. Fresh roses and baby's breath brightened the altar. The acolytes, two black cherubs dressed in coats and ties, were applauded as they stood on tiptoe to light the candles. The text was read with deep sincerity by those who believed every word and lived it the best they could.

Suddenly, Tony was escorting me to the altar. What was going on? Tony had brought his entire family into the church membership. No Annapolis bride marching up the aisle under crossed swords had a more handsome or precious escort.

I knew every person we passed in the pews "by heart," had been in their homes, knew their pains and their blessings. Almost the entire congregation had accepted Christ and been baptized at the altar where I now stood. And in the quiet times of my own personal pain or joy, I had stormed the gates of heaven at this same altar.

Phil Austin, our unpaid minister of music, eighty-three and still going on twenty, musically and spiritually brilliant, came forward. His sure, steady hand was trembling. Through tears he told me that the church had voted unanimously to dedicate the new youth center and parlor to me and call it "The Rose Room."

The bronze plaque read:

THE ROSE ROOM
dedicated to the
GLORY OF GOD AND IN HONOR OF
DR. ROSE GRINDHEIM SIMS, PASTOR

In 1984 she came to a closing church. She established first an outreach program with food, clothes, medical service. She started Sunday school classes, UMW, youth group, singles, senior games and activities such as cooking and writing classes. She brought gospel sings, groups, revival ministers. Using all volunteer labor she raised money to build a debt-free sanctuary, mission, the Rose Room and Education Center. In 1985 and again each year it was proclaimed that Trilby

United Methodist Church was by ratio the leader in professions of faith in Florida. In 1987 the Methodist Church declared Trilby national CHURCH AFLAME. In 1988 Dr. Rose tied for first place for the Circuit Rider Award, the highest honor given to an outstanding minister for church growth in the United States.

The formula for her success: W O R K

Why had they written work? Why not prayer or preaching? At every growth seminar I said, "A church is like my house when it is a mess. I know there is hard work ahead, and I am as lazy as the next person. I know I cannot stand the mess and plan to clean it up soon. Until I do, my husband is crabby, my job rotten and I am a lousy cook. Once I put honest sweat and toil into it, my husband's looks improve, I have a super job and I am a gourmet cook." The Trilby folks were right. Lots of preachers with similar theology had mighty different results. Perhaps work made the difference. Winning souls is hard, back-breaking work.

Every academic trophy I had won, every degree I had earned, even conference membership itself, paled in comparison with the tribute I received that morning.

I was expected to respond. "If you knew how much joy I have had serving this church, you would start charging me for being your pastor. All my life I have sought to reach the minds, hearts and souls of my fellow man with the just fear of God and the love of their souls. I have some very precious children and daughter- and sons-in-law and grandchildren. I hope that some day, maybe long after I am gone, they will bring their grandchildren to see this temple raised to God and share their heritage."

I meant it from the deepest recesses of my being. The separation from the children had at times been unbearable and crushing. We had grown up such a close family. But to see my life work so deeply engraved in both mortar and mind for the next generation obliterated every sacrifice. I had often included in my morning prayers, "And please let something happen here today that is not in the bulletin." Today it certainly had.

Jim's hug primed the pump. The entire congregation, including sturdy, solid men with scratchy whiskers and tears streaming down their weather-beaten cheeks, said, in Florida "Cracker" talk, "Come here and let me hug on your neck."

Children in all colors and sizes wanted a hug. Young people who knew a phone call at midnight would provide safety, young couples struggling with two-career marriages, the rich and the poor, with tears of love and joy streaming down their cheeks wrote their liturgy of love, their own sermon on spiritual freedom.

The seminary professor who once cautioned that familiarity breeds contempt did not understand rural churches.

Out here we are just plain "Florida Cracker Home Folks." We share each others' cooking at potlucks, and we like the lifting gospel hymns we pick. We invite the preacher and our neighbors home for dinner after church, the guys pitch horseshoes, the young folks pitch woo and the ladies cook great pots of red beans and rice, hominy grits and gravy. Keep those folks at arm's length and build a church? Forget it!

"But," the professor had argued, "it may be risky to let them see you, warts and all." But who ever said God was finished perfecting his saints?

I silently prayed for the United Methodist Church which had yet to discover that being on the Board of Ministry does not provide a dues card to indict as disposable the small evangelical church or its pastor.

Dear Jesus, I prayed, *make the world see what a cataclysmic, catastrophic calamity it is to throw this priceless antique jewel on the trash heap of Wesley's worldwide vision, just at the zero hour for America. Let me have conference membership so that I can wave the palms of hope for all my downtrodden sisters and brothers who, by their faithfulness to almighty God and his church, have earned a triumphant entrance.*

I pronounced the benediction. The organist and Norm's silver trumpet played the postlude, "My Hope is Built."

Today was Palm Sunday. Crucifixion may be just ahead, but I had learned to think of the crucifi xion with great joy because it meant that resurrection was next.

14

Mangrove Trees in the Moonlight

Early Monday morning we headed for Atlanta's Hyatt Regency Hotel and the Circuit Rider Awards banquet.

The azaleas, dogwoods and irises, which had long since come and gone in Florida, were in full bloom in Atlanta. At the awards banquet, all three ministers who tied for the award spoke. Kirbyjon H. Caldwell, pastor of Windsor Village United Methodist Church of Houston, spoke first, then C. Philip Hinerman of Park Avenue United Methodist Church in Minneapolis. I spoke last.

"Some people say, 'Seeing is believing.' I say believing is seeing. I believe both are true, so I have brought some slides," I said. In a few brief moments I flashed slides of our pilgrimage on a huge overhead screen.

I was saying to America, "It can happen anywhere and must happen everywhere." I have done what you asked me to do, Oscar. The task is finished.

The next Sunday was Mother's Day and a cherished day when

each of the children touched base. A brilliant floral bouquet came from Jim's only son, Jim Jr. and his family. The card read, "We're so glad that you are our Mom." My oldest daughter and husband, both physicians, were at Disney World. My heart ached to see the grandchildren. Ben's blond hair, quick wit and fierce competitive athletic prowness reminded me of his Viking heritage. Ann is a fine musician and aspires to be a writer.

Gaylie, our second daughter, had earlier developed the music department at Auburn University in Montgomery, Alabama, where she met and married David, a fine devoted fellow professor. They were both well-settled now in their careers of music and government. Her Nordic beauty is a mirror image of her father, Oscar.

Our youngest, Lee, an actuary, had planted herself squarely in the Washington, D.C. political scene. Her work sent her to represent the American Psychological Society and the College of Nuclear Medicine.

Rob will always suffer from early deprivation. But, I am equally proud of his skill with horses and his faithfulness to his job as a stable boy on a fine horsefarm. He is kind and generous and a great and faithful friend.

I was delighted that Ron's troubled teen and prison years were behind him. He seemed happier now. Married to Cathy, they have two precious children, Victoria Rose and Ron. The many long hours spent storming heaven's gate and the pledge to always love unconditionally had its rewards. Ron was working in building trades.

May brought three phone calls from the bishop. The wheels were in motion. On May 22 I met with the District Board of Ministry, which passed me unanimously.

The bishop asked Jim and me to meet him in his office the next day so he could go over any possible snag I might encounter the next Sunday evening during a meeting he had requested with the Florida Conference Board of Ministry.

We chatted about Trilby. I told him the new building was up and debt free. He had said before, "Trilby is one of the most remarkable achievements in my forty-three years of ministry." Now he asked to come and dedicate it in August. He was retiring September 1. "We will be packing, and I have all the Sundays in August free." I was elated and knew the Trilby people would be ecstatic. It would be his final sermon in Florida. We would have a country church farewell . . . not fancy fixin's, just dinner on the grounds. We'd invite all the neighboring churches and their choirs and sing out of the old Cokesbury hymnal. My struggle for conference membership would be over tomorrow and a new day would be dawning for others similarly oppressed.

My district superintendent was there with us. In his presence, the bishop declared, "There is no question in my mind that you have to have had conference membership since you were ordained in 1973." Once again he reiterated his affirmation, "This is no longer a matter of Dr. Rose Sims; this is a matter of right and justice for all clergy."

He rose from his huge swivel chair and stepped from behind the enormous mahogany desk. It was morning in my heart and the golden sun was rising; its brilliance was streaming across the altar of every Methodist church in the world.

I wanted to hug him. I had given hundreds of hugs to hundreds of God's people, but I had never hugged a bishop. Besides, he was too big to hug. His nearly seven foot frame towered over me as did his towering Christian spirit.

I was grateful I had gone to Trilby, if for no other reason than to meet Bishop Hunt. I am eternally grateful for having known him, enormously grieved that he has retired and left us.

I pledged then and there that, with the strength that conference membership would afford, I would never forget the enormous pain of those who were powerless. I would lovingly work for justice until it happened for all evangelicals. Bishop Hunt, by his intervention, showed that "justice and right" is not just a cliche in the Social Justice Code of our United Methodist *Discipline*, but a living, breathing reality for all Methodists.

My appointment with the Board of Ministry was for seven-thirty that Sunday night. I was early but was not called before them until eight-thirty. I sensed before I got in that something was awry—that a mighty power struggle was raging to determine who holds the key to Methodist pulpits. The bishop had sent both of the district superintendents I had worked under to testify positively on my behalf, and we chatted about the weather.

The Board members did not acknowledge Jim or me . . . although we were fellow pilgrims in ministry, they were acting like strangers. I don't believe they meant to do this, but it is a complaint I have heard over and over again.

Having taught psychology and counseling all my life, I was no novice at conflict management. I called upon those skills now. These men were my colleagues, my brothers, called by my God. Now, strangely, they were bristling adversaries.

I began by thanking them for taking time out of a busy Sunday. I said I was sure they were weary after preaching then driving long distances; some of them must have traveled far. I acknowledged this was an unusual meeting and I was deeply grateful.

Then the questioning began.

"Who called this meeting?"

"I believe the bishop did."

"Are you sure you didn't call it? Haven't you had other meetings about other topics with the bishop this spring? What were they about?"

"I believe that is confidential."

"You are avoiding the issue."

"I'm sorry. I didn't mean to be evasive. It was about a private matter. Since you asked, we left five thousand dollars for a Grindheim-Sims award to be given this year to a rural pastor."

"What else did you discuss?"

"We discussed ways my estate could best be invested for the rural Methodist Church."

"What are your sermon topics, and how do you get so many people to come to church?"

"Most in my congregation are brand new Christians. They need such a variety of sermons. They drive long distances of their own volition to worship and work." I left it at that.

"What were the negative findings in your psychological report?"

"Have you read it?"

"No." I was amazed. Discipline 731 says the BOM must carefully study each candidate's file.

"It was highly complimentary. I honestly can't remember anything negative."

"Do you think you are perfect? If not, what are your faults?"

"I fail God over and over. My weakness is that I spend so much time building buildings that I neglect my spiritual life. I am determined to remedy that by reading, for the first time in my life, the Bible completely through in a year."

"Are you driven? Too intense?"

"I am called. I work in an area where there is enormous poverty and pain. The love of Christ compels me. I believe America is truly in a crisis."

"What do you feel is the purpose of the church?"

"To win the lost and make disciples of all men."

"How do you handle people in the church who dislike you, who disagree with you and get in your way?"

"We are in a loving, caring church. I thanked my people from the pulpit this morning that to my knowledge there has never been an unkind or critical word spoken in our church. We have had many difficult decisions to make. We have struggled with many new ideas and visions, but I have never once left a meeting which did not end with hugging and harmony."

"What have you failed at, and how do you deal with rejection?"

"The Tampa *Tribune* asked me that same question recently in an interview. It was the first time I realized that I had never once thought about Trilby failing. I am not being naive, or dealing flippantly with your question. I have failed God many times. He has never failed me. I just don't believe God's promises are geared for failure."

"Rejection—What evidence do you have that you can deal with that? I am sure you must be angry that you have served this long without conference membership."

My integrity was at stake and that was far more important than conference membership. I tried to think about how I felt the day I was put out in the cold after my years of service in Missouri. Angry? Bitter? Retaliatory? No! Just very, very sad for my beloved dying United Methodist Church and for America so in need of Christ.

"I believe my record shows that I have responded by being faithful to God's call."

I was told to wait outside. The night was dark except for the lone evening star which twinkled brightly in a cloudless pitch-black sky. I searched for Jim. He had just come through a surgery, after which, thank God, we had heard that blessed pronouncement, "benign." For three long hours tonight he had faithfully waited. He had fallen asleep on a bench in the shadows of the great First United Methodist Church whose steeple pointed a finger skyward.

He was coming toward me. I ran to meet him. His arms held me close, just as I knew God's everlasting arms had held me through death, despair and victory.

The moon was rising, big and full of golden promise in the midst of the dark, dark night as we stepped back into the meeting room.

One by one the Board members slinked by us without a single polite "good night." That's how I knew the verdict.

They had sent the youngest pastor in the group to fetch me. There were only five Board members left in the huge empty room with its unwashed blackboard that still had the morning's Sunday school Scripture written on it. The clock on the wall said it was nearly eleven.

The chairperson spoke. "It is the decision of the Board of Ordained Ministry that we not recommend you for associate membership at this time. The board affirms your potential for ministry and notes your many strengths. It is our purpose to assist you in perfecting your gifts for ministry and to this end the board is requiring you to fulfill the following contingency:

"Successfully complete a unit of Clinical Pastoral Education at Lakeland General Hospital in which you make relevant 'areas of concern' a part of your program agenda. Have your CPE Supervisor address these concerns in a report which you will release to the conference registrar. The areas of concern listed below will help you understand the action of the Board and also serve as an agenda for your contingency. This must be addressed prior to your again being properly before the Board. The concerns are based on comments and questions by the Board members during and after your interviews, and may reveal misconceptions. Nevertheless, they reflect the basis of the Board's decision.

1. Not seen as emotionally available.
2. Seen as evasive in responding to questions from the Board.
3. Difficulty when not getting your way.
4. Perceived as overly intense and driven."

Now it was my turn to respond.

"Have you read the excellent evaluation I got from the Clinical Pastoral Education Report I did to fulfill CPE requirements for the Missouri East Conference?"

"No."

"Since I have some background in psychology, would you be offended if I proffered a professional opinion? It seems that the concerns you list are more psychological in nature than counseling-oriented. I believe the report of my psychological evaluation would shed the light you need. Have you read it?"

"No."

When I took the test the BOM psychologist had searched for someone competent to give the test. I had given hundreds of them which alone would disqualify me. He must have known that but I took them. I then was sent to Dr. Bosbyshell for the oral evaluation. He looked at my record and said I was as qualified to do this as he . He told me his assistant had some personal problems and asked if I would share with her while he wrote the report.

In giving me the report he said, "You rank above ninety-nine percent of any ministerial candidate I have ever evaluated." In part the record read, "With her background, training and experience, she is as aware of and as experienced as the examiner. She is a well-balanced, extroverted, thinking, feeling personality type. She is capable, responsible, executive-type woman who has held positions of leadership in which she functions with a clear sense of responsibility and careful consideration of peoples' needs and concerns." It concluded, "She is a mature, wise, competent woman, truly experienced, a capable pastor who should function well for many years." Dr. Bosbyshell marveled that they required the tests but did not bother to read them.

Bishop Hunt had written: "Dr. Sims' work is the most remarkable ministry of my long years in the episcopacy and ministry." I knew my records were flawless. But, they had not read them. Little wonder so many competent pastors were turned down repeatedly while others whose churches were dying passed so easily.

Bishop Wilke in his book, *And Are We Yet Alive*, had written,

> Our sickness is more serious than we at first suspected. We are in trouble, you and I, and our United Methodist Church. We thought we were just drifting, like a sailboat on a dreamy day. Instead, we are wasting away like a leukemia victim whose blood transfusions no longer work. Once we were a Wesleyan revival fired by the Spirit. Now we are listless, tired, fueled only by nostalgia, putting one foot ahead of the other

> like a tired old man who remembers, but can no longer perform.

Why? This year we had hemorrhaged away seventy thousand members. I had just been made the pawn in a colossal power struggle to control the pulpits and theology of the United Methodist church. The players had been the bishop and the Board of Ministry. The bishop had lost.

"Thank you very much for seeing me," I told the remaining BOM members. "I know you are weary. My husband just had surgery, and it has been a long night for him, too."

One lone man stepped forward and reached out a hand. He was pastor of the great high steeple church in St. Petersburg.

"Dr. Sims, I just want you to know I am ashamed to be part of this Board of Ministry tonight. You are a fascinating lady, and Tampa First Church has never ceased singing your praises since you preached there. I would love to have you on staff."

"Thank you so much. I really appreciate that. You have no idea the similar offers I have had. Many of them have been tempting. But I feel that anyone would snatch your offer in a minute and almost nobody would go to Trilby and Lacoochee. That's why I think they need me and that's why I'm here tonight."

On the way home, Jim and I rolled down the top of his convertible and let the night air blow fresh on an open wound. We wound our way silently along the moonlit ribbon of road redundant with pine, cabbage palms and palmetto. The red mangrove trees, standing on stilts, looked like crouching creatures.

> Sad, how only naturalists admire the mangrove trees. They seem to me to have almost an animal-like gentle spirit and intelligence. . . . They tiptoe forward, grimly holding each bit of gained ground. . . . They are usually the first vicitms of bulldozers. (Ernest Lyons, quoted by Sidney Lanter, *Florida, Its Scenery, Climate and History.*)

I knew that hidden deep in the cypress swamps the proud American eagle slept with his head securely tucked under one protecting wing. Tomorrow he would fly screaming a wild "aa-oo-ee" at the pandemonium that was turning the last frontier into trailer villages. I felt a strong kinship to the eagle and to God's silent night.

15

Power that Struts—or Serves?

I was loathe to face the Annual Conference, which would be speaking for Florida Methodism in just eight short hours. This would be Bishop Hunt's swan song. I had no intelligent explanation for those who would ask, "Why didn't you get membership?" I knew it was now or never.

The *Discipline* says that a petition may be put on the floor and the clergy, in executive session, could vote to override the Board of Ministry's decision. I prepared a draft of the petition and consulted Dr. Martha Rutland-Wallace, who headed the Florida Commission on Status and Role of Women. She said she would read the petition on the conference floor. Jim took the day off and Phil Austin, Trilby's lay leader and minister of music, called to say he wanted to represent the church.

But I did not want to circumvent Bishop Hunt. I learned he had been calling my name on the conference floor. Trilby was to be honored as first in the state in our category in professions of faith.

I opened the door of the great Branscomb Hall. The room was dark; inside they were showing a movie about Florida Advance Specials. I slipped around the huge auditorium and found a tiny door marked "platform." It was open and the bishop's white head shone like a halo in the darkness. We had thirty minutes before the film would be over. The bishop took me into his tiny improvised office, bare but for his briefcase. He read the petition I had written and said it looked good. He said he would take it to his secretary at noon and have her type it letter-perfect. "I will also research if there is any clause in jurisdictional law which prohibits the Annual Conference from overriding the Board of Ministry's decision," he added. His final comment to me as he was called back to the floor was, "We will do all we can. This is not a matter of Rose Sims, but of right and justice."

I met the bishop at one o'clock to pick up the revised copy of the petition. "There is nothing I can do," Bishop Hunt said, shaking his head and handing me a jurisdictional ruling the BOM must have given him dated October 30, 1982. It later proved this ruling had been obsolete for several years. The petition was indeed legal but never presented.

I sought solitude on the manicured lawn by the lake that skirted the campus. I had to read what the bishop had handed me and to pray and think.

Slowly, deliberately I read the carefully underlined jurisdictional ruling. On October 30, 1982 the late Bishop Marjorie S. Matthews, the very first woman ever elected bishop, struck the death knell for my being accepted on the floor of the conference when she made the following motion, which was sustained. It read:

> A candidate applying for admission to an Annual Conference must meet all the requirements of the *Discipline,* including recommendations by the Board of Ministry. Without that recommendation, no person is properly before the Annual Conference.

I thought to myself, "Methodist Discipline is law for Methodists, but it would take a Philadelphia lawyer to interpret it."

I wondered: Does the Board of Ministry have no checks and balances? Has the powerful United Methodist Church abandoned its "justice" to a handful of clergy who do not even do their homework and who disregard competency as they play God with the sacred call to the ministry and the holy orders of the church? Are the bishop and the annual conference as powerless as the lowliest evangelical seeking confirmation?

If a minister is discriminated against in such secular matters as salary, advancement, job security, pension, etc., if he or she is denied rights that are guaranteed and commonly understood and ordinarily practiced among all citizens of our country, does the separation of church and state put the church above the law?

The world is sick at heart about a power that struts; it is hungry for a power that serves. The church is weak and anemic because it lives beneath its privilege of powers.

That night Bishop Hunt gave his last "Hurrah."

He read his text and began. "Then I saw a new heaven and a new earth. . . . Behold, I make all things new" (Revelation 21:1, 5, KJV).

With keen intellect and powerful Holy Spirit preaching, he mingled joy, hope and longing for a new heaven and a new earth:

> I am grateful to my church. Across forty-seven years of ministry I have served as associate pastor, pastor, college president and bishop. The largest and most important special task has come this quadrennium when I had the honor of chairing the Committee on our Theological Task; and perhaps the greatest sense of exultation I have experienced was the moment in St. Louis early this month when the General Conference adopted its new doctrinal statement by a vote of more than 9 to 1.

The bishop should have been weary, but he looked younger, more alive and refreshed than I had ever seen him.

Like an old sea captain, he was at the pilot's wheel, turning the bow of that great vessel clearly toward harbor.

> One's personal faith in the Lord Jesus Christ is finally the most significant ingredient in his or her resume. I am not speaking of your or my theology but of something far deeper, that interior impulse of Christian assurance that wells up from the deep places within us, and tells us, even in the darkest of nights, that we belong to "God and God belongs to us."
>
> An old Scandinavian legend declares that God builds a bridge joining earth and heaven. The day of the Lord is not passed, but yet to come. There is a power no adversary can conquer, a light no darkness can dim. Great is thy faithfulness, Lord unto me. Amen.

My old Scandinavian had said exactly that, many long years ago, and for that hope, I had worn his mantle.

The conference was over for me. The ordination ceremony would be too painful to attend. I stopped at the Lakeland General Hospital and talked with Chaplain Burrows about fulfilling my CPE requirements there. He inquired about my education, my experience and my present assignment. He suggested I not sit in on his lectures, which were intended for beginning freshmen at the local unaccredited school. Besides, the last time the BOM sent a clergy through his program the student was rejected again. He said he would be delighted to have me working on a floor, but he saw little validity for the contingencies.

Phone calls to a few fallen comrades confirmed my worst fears. Some evangelicals who had finally gotten conference membership were so long in getting it that they feared to lift their bruised heads. Those who did not have it feared reprisal and worked as thieves in the night or were simply swept under the rug and vanished.

I wanted to know what reasons were discussed by the BOM before it rejected my last plea for recognition of my ordination. I called the one gentleman who had apologized to me after the meeting.

"What was said at the BOM meeting? Why was I turned down?" I asked.

"I wish I could answer that," he replied. "I have never been able to give a definition to the cumulative decision of the Board. . . . They felt someone (the bishop) was pushing them into accepting you. I cannot say why they did not accept you. I can say it was a frustrating experience . . . I am totally impotent on the Board. Would that I were not. I had the personal feeling that you should have been elected . . . I don't think there was any personal criticism of you in that setting. I couldn't say what was going on in the minds of individuals. If I knew I would answer. I have great admiration of you. You are a remarkable lady. The whole thing happened, and I don't think there is anything any of us can do. I know I can't. I was on the Board sixteen years and I could not understand the ones they passed."

After that conversation I knew the core of the issue is a *power struggle* for control of the United Methodist Church, not me. The BOM wanted to prove that even one of our most powerful bishops in America has no power to make appointments or select candidates for the pulpits he is supposed to fill.

The laity needs to know that they have abandoned power rightfully theirs. Few even dream that the BOM holds the key to Methodist pulpits and hence to the denomination's theology. I believe this is the best kept secret in Methodism and the answer to why liberation theology and liberalism are flourishing and the United Methodist church is dying.

I was just a pawn. My work, ministry, ordination and test results didn't matter. That meeting with the Board had nothing to do with *me*. . . nor competency, accountability, nor even very much with discrimination. It had to do with *power* to fill the pulpits of Methodism. It had to do with seminaries that turn out pastors whose vision is far from Wesley's. It had to do with impotent, voiceless laity who have been told and who believe they have no recourse but to pay apportionments and the pastor's salary even if their church is being killed.

The laity comprises 99.5 percent of Methodist membership. Clergy comprise the other half percent . At Annual Conference where United Methodist business is conducted, laypersons have one vote, clergy one vote. This means that half of one percent of Methodists have power to make fifty percent of the decisions. Worse yet, the Board of Ministry is composed entirely of clergy (in 1988 the Florida BOM voted to let one layperson without a vote observe). Ironically, the BOM comprise a minute part of the one half of one percent of the Methodist Church, yet they have one hundred percent control of the pulpits of the church. They can exclude any persons or viewpoints they wish. Competency, accountability, requirements of the *Discipline*, soul-winning, the Pastor-Parish Committee, the wish of the churches, even the recommendation of the bishop can be totally ignored. Unfortunately, the clergy they have admitted have presided over the near demise of the United Methodist Church.

No where else but in the United Methodist Church do the employees write their own blank checks. The laity until now has felt helpless when an incompetent pastor was assigned to their church, and were told they are powerless with no option but to pay the salary and hope for better leadership next appointment.

It is the zero hour to change this and it can be done. First, a petition to General Conference could demand that the Board of Ministry be composed of a majority of laity. Those who pay the salary, who have built the churches and who have the vested interest in their survival could demand that hiring be in the hands of the employers. Secondly, the church sets the salary of the pastor. By refusing to pay the salary for an incompetent pastor, they would be casting their vote for change. True, this would have to be done on a large scale and as part of a powerful revolt, but I believe it is what Wesley envisioned would be where the leadership of the church rested.

As I pondered what to do next, a dear friend from Missouri, Dr. Mel West, suggested that when all else failed I should read Matthew 18:15-17:

> If your brother sins against you, go and show him his fault, just between the two of you. If he listens to you, you have won your brother over. But if he will not listen, take one or two others along so that 'every matter may be established by the testimony of two or three witnesses.' If he refuses to listen to them, tell it to the church; and if he refuses to listen even to the church, treat him as you would a pagan or a tax collector.

It was no longer just my struggle. The struggle was between the liberals and the evangelicals, between Methodism's most powerful bishop and a clergy group determined to perpetuate by any means, including discrimination and injustice, the theology which was making the church extinct. It had been Wesley's struggle in his day, and now it was the bishop's struggle, and the struggle of all those seeking to revive the church.

Jim suggested I call Judy Kavenaugh, who had gained national acclaim in the very difficult and painful landmark case regarding the Ray children who had Aids Related Complex. We needed to see if Matthew 18:15-17 had been exhausted.

I made an appointment and went to see her.

Ms. Kavenaugh's smile was genuine as she reached for my hand.

She looked at the material I gave her and asked precise questions. She spoke of her own Episcopal Church. Her keen intellect, quiet dignity and skill with words gave me confidence that this attorney would indeed fight for justice.

She asked about my family and I about hers. She had five children. Her career had been as fraught with struggles for survival as mine.

I explained that I would only seek justice if it complied with Matthew 18:15-17. She agreed to take the case on a contingency basis—

if there were a case. But she had fought so many cases for free. She would have to pay her staff to help her research my papers, the *Discipline* and all the loving ways justice could be done within the system of the United Methodist Church. I left a check.

For the very first time since retiring and turning in his Air Force uniform, Jim had six entire weeks off. Too many people had said, "I wonder what will happen to Trilby when Rose leaves." To that end, I had carefully trained leadership which was now mature and ready to test.

I asked the church for a five week vacation. A few asked, "Can we combine some classes, cut out the choir and the calling and let the church coast for a while?"

It had become crystal clear to me that this is why churches die. The plaque on the Rose Room wall was right: *Work*. This was their chance to show that the church was bigger than any one person. I challenged them to have twenty in the choir when I came back, to include the youth in the choir, to organize one new Sunday school class and to begin a home Bible study. Their future, not mine depended on it. The closer the time came for our leaving, the more leadership rose to the occasion.

Our motor home was packed, the last service was over, and we were ready to leave on Monday morning. I was reading the Sunday *Tribune* travel section: "Win a Cruise to the Caribbean," "Lugano is Worth a Second Trip," and "Vacation Breezes Beckon to the Tropical Isles."

Down in the corner, I spotted a most surprising headline: "The tiny community of Trilby in Northeastern Pasco County is clinging to life, but hope for a revival rests on its United Methodist Church. See page two." I did.

The headline read, "Methodist Church Is Reviving Trilby." Big as life, there was our old church and a map of Pasco County. Trilby, at long last, was really on the map.

George Lane, a roving reporter, had intended to write a story on Trilby's poverty. He was startled to find, amid the squalor, the lovely Trilby United Methodist Church, flowers abloom, fountain playing in the sunshine and its long slender steeple pointing heavenward.

Some teenagers were deep in conversation while seated on the gold and white marble benches in the courtyard shadowed by the magnificent Italian stone sanctuary.

"You know anything about this church? Any way I could see the inside?" the reporter asked.

"No sweat." They slicked off a screen, climbed in the window, and told him all about "their church." As a result, Trilby was now being acclaimed with more space in the travel section of Tampa's leading paper than all those far away places.

The kids shouldn't have been in the church. I had turned my head the other way and tried to pretend I didn't know that some of those kids slept in the church when they got kicked out at home by a drunken father or an irate stepmother, or if they feared sexual abuse. I had found homes for many, but I had also left blankets and the mission porch unlocked. Trilby United Methodist Church was a safe place in an unsafe world.

The roving reporter described Trilby's story, warts and all.

Then on a hopeful note he added, "Perhaps Trilby's rapidly growing United Methodist church is the cornerstone of the town's renewed spirit of vim, vigor and vitality."

He ended with "Once the rural church was the strength of America, and the Methodist Church in Trilby and hundreds of other towns like this are fertile soil for the church's rebirth in Florida, America, and maybe the world. What is happening at the Trilby Methodist Church offers new hope. When the world is at its worst, that is when the church must be at its best."

It was Monday morning and five long, lazy carefree weeks stretched before us. We would lazily follow the Withlacoochee River, stopping at a little catfish restaurant for breakfast. By Saturday we would be in Kansas City to see Jim's grandson receive his Eagle Scout Award. I had stocked the motor home with a supply of good books, and Jim was checking the locks when the phone rang.

"Let her ring," I begged. We did, and it rang and rang and rang. As earnestly as I had resisted my first call, I wanted to be rid of the awesome load now resting on our shoulders.

Finally, I picked up the phone.

"This is Judy Kavenaugh, and here is what I have found. The question is whether civil rights extend to the church. Under some circumstances, the church has autonomy and can discriminate where it is a matter of their faith. For instance, discrimination against nuns is included in the vows they take."

Judy continued, "The Methodist Church, however, is far different. You are governed by a *Discipline,* a contract which guarantees you equal rights and ordains both women and men. Constitutional prohibition of discrimination in church matters is very strong. There is no precedent. This would be the first case, but I think it will fly.

"The way to approach it is to secularize the church structure, not the faith or the religion itself. The church is to be treated no differently than a private business as long as it espouses equality. It cannot claim to fall back on its religious tenets when its own religious discipline denies it the right to do what it is doing.

"If we secularize the Methodist Church, then we can envision a scenario in which the court will say, 'Yes, you're right, we will treat the church much like we would treat anyone who is conducting illegal discrimination.' Once the court agrees, we have liability. Nobody has tried it, but I can see where a court would then look to see if we had some internal remedy. The courts are reluctant to act. They always look first to see if there is an administrative remedy.

"We have to establish that you have exhausted any internal process within the Methodist Church and that it would be futile to pursue any further action.

"When it becomes a typical discrimination case, we can get the court to take religion out and put justice in. We can get by the little parochial group you have had to deal with and have you considered on the merits of your qualifications.

"What we are proposing is to prepare a demand letter to the church. If they reject it, you could go to court. That is what I intend to have waiting for you when you get to Kansas City."

I had just received the Circuit Rider Award, I was not financially dependent on salary, I had better than average education and God had crowned his work in my ministry. This decision could destroy all that. I would be acclaimed an aggressive female, a "women's libber." It would be discussed in the news, from the pulpits and by those who said Methodists were disobedient to God when they ordained women. I had been reappointed to Trilby for this year. But next year they could retire me.

It was past time to go. With Air Force precision, Jim had made the decision. Already he was warming up the motor home.

Quickly I typed a note to the bishop. I enclosed a quote from Leslie Weatherhead and slipped both into a long church envelope.

When his church was destroyed by Nazi bombs, Weatherhead wrote from the midst of that destruction,

> When I am hot and rebellious, bitter and cynical and sarcastic, when it seems evil can win in the world and the battle is strong, when it seems as though pride possesses all the high places and greatness belongs to those who can grab the most, when it seems that faith is mocked and humility is trodden in the dust, when pity seems weakness and sympathy folly, when a foul egotism rises up within me bidding me assert myself, serve my own interest and look out for number one . . . then, O my God, as I listen down the corridor of the years for the voice of the Almighty, may I hear the gentle splashing of water in a basin and see the Son of God washing the disciples' feet.

I wanted Bishop Hunt to know I wanted justice only as it was scripturally mandated, and I would seek it only "towel and basin in hand." The bishop would preach his last sermon of a long and fruitful ministry at the August 21 dedication of the Rose Room and youth center. It was a high honor, and one I did not want to jeopardize. I knew the bishop was above recrimination.

We rode in silence, northward, up the four-lane asphalt ribbon that is Highway 98, past the gigantic yellow and black sign where the newly hatched chicken still proclaimed daily, "Start life anew at Trilby United Methodist Church," past the "Catch the Spirit" signs that read four miles, then two miles, then half a block. We had passed the neat millionaire homes of Dade City and had driven by the shanties, the Starlite Bar, the drive-in theater playing *Free Love* and the motel where a brilliant college student had taken cyanide. As we passed this citadel of sin where our kids lay by the wayside, sexually and spiritually wounded, it was good to know Trilby Methodists had not "passed by on the other side."

Jim broke the silence. "Since we are finally tourists, suppose you mail that letter at Florida's highly acclaimed tourist center, Trilby."

We turned at the blinking light, just as the "Catch the Spirit" sign suggested.

There in the golden summer, just as the Tampa *Tribune's* travel section had described it, was Trilby, Florida. Just two lone buildings, the Post Office and the Trilby United Methodist Church. On each, flying high in God's sky, was Old Glory: two identical flags representing church and state, with nothing but a ribbon of country road dividing them—or was it joining them?

Jim parked in the shade of a magnificent old oak tree laden with Spanish moss. He reached for the letter. "May I read it?" he asked. He read it aloud slowly and deliberately.

> Dear Bishop Hunt,
>
> Thanks so much for your willingness to be with us August 21. The church is ecstatic, and while I said, "We won't put on no airs," they are planning some "fancy folderol." We would like to have you speak in the morning. We will invite neighboring churches for a Country Gospel Sing.
>
> Jim and I send our deepest appreciation for your advocacy. We are aware of all you did. You are a giant in faith, in love and human compassion.
>
> In the far-flung, lonely, desolate corners of God's harvest field stand reapers, whose enviable dedication and devotion to almighty God haunts my days and fills my sleepless nights.
>
> For them, justice is right. Many have not had my enviable opportunities for personal happiness, success, education and financial security.
>
> I do not believe justice can wait. Jim has paid $5,000 for the best legal advice possible to see if all of us have exhausted Matthew 18:15-17. If not, we will proceed with haste, while your strong voice is still heard in Florida. I hope it is an opportunity for all of us to do something significant that will last for eternity. Without justice and right, the church for which we have lived, will die.
>
> Lovingly in Christ,
> Jim and Rose Sims

Jim is the most peace loving man I know, yet he spent twenty years serving his country at home and abroad, on front lines and in fox holes. Yes, Jim had put his life on the line for justice and right and equality and freedom.

In the shade of God's everlasting arms and that mighty oak, he sealed the letter tight as if to punctuate a long, long sentence. A majestic American bald eagle sat delicately perched on the tiny iron cross atop the old church steeple. He lifted his enormous wings and flew high into the golden sun. As his great gray and gold wingtips cast their shadow across the church, the post office and the tiny county road joining them, he gave a wild, victorious cry. High in the sky, defying extinction, he flew God-ward, soaring higher and higher with seemingly effortless grace until he was safe and secure, beyond the reach of man's mindless efforts toward his destruction.

Jim mailed the letter.

16

'Deliverance Will Come'

The next five weeks were unplanned. With no schedule, we would just laze our way up the river and stop where we wanted. We'd explore America at the grass roots, camp by its waysides and rethink America's dilemma. We had discovered how to make it happen anywhere, but what would it take to make it happen everywhere? What had happened to those churches we had served over the years? We decided to visit them and as many others as possible. Cool evening breezes, the last we were to know for weeks, sang us to sleep.

Crossing the state line, unprecedented 112- and 113-degree weather scorched us state after state over all the parched, drought-ridden Central Plains. We found even more drought and despair in many of the churches we visited, yet in others the seed planted was bearing an abundant harvest, tenfold or a hundredfold.

We began, as does each good research study, with an untested hypothesis. Was it possible that those churches which did not decline as they changed pastors were those with a strong, vibrant watch-dog evangelical *laity* guarding the pulpit through one appointment after the other? Was the key the *laity* who were trained to be soul-winners, who by precept, vigilance and resistance to false doctrine practiced practical soul-winning and demanded the same from their clergy? If a pastor wanted to make sure a church survived, was the secret not just to make converts but to mold those converts into disciples who are not totally dependent on leadership to make the church grow?

Another good question is why Methodists who bemoan the demise of the church have cut from their accredited list of seminaries the very ones whose graduates produce church growth. There are few evangelical survivors on the accredited list and their graduates are too often shunned. Many United Methodist semin ary students tell of continuing academic coercion and discrimination against evangelical seminarians. All seminaries are not alike. If seminaries which produce "growth-oriented" pastors could be pinpointed, then Pastor-Parish Relations Committees, once they raise their bruised heads and demand their rights as more and more clergy seek fewer available pulpits, could ask for those specific graduates and be persistent in seeing that they get them in their pulpits.

In five weeks Jim and I traveled across forty-three years of memories by visiting places we had once called home. I had never been back to most of the churches. I heard again the laughter of long-grown children on Christmas mornings. The remains of a tree house Oscar had lovingly built was still up in the old mulberry tree. Those who had been youth presidents were now grandmothers. Many saints were gone. Some parsonages stood empty, rented out beside closed and decaying churches. Other churches radiated life and vitality and hope.

Never once in those clergy wife days had I visualized myself in Oscar's pulpit. Why should I? It had always been enough to walk by his side, stretching to keep up with his ten-league spiritual boots. Now with joy and a bit of trepidation I ascended each hallowed spot where he had given his last best hurrah. With tears of joy overwhelming my grateful heart I realized the vast inheritance to which I had fallen heir—an America which Lincoln called the world's best hope and the vital church on Main Street, which has been the backbone of this young nation.

I looked back over my own wonderfully joyous pilgrimage with a marvelous peace as I saw at last clearly and surely the reason why my thorn in the flesh had been conference membership. If almighty

God, using a woman past sixty—without conference membership, buildings, parsonage, congregation, guaranteed salary or appointment—in the third world areas of America, could make it happen so joyously, then truly anyone could make it happen anywhere. Yes, it could happen in any denomination, with anyone with nothing but a sure call. Anyone with nothing but the unadulterated Word of God and his eternal promises could see it happen. That is how our country church had been built long ago.

Those circuit-riding preachers had braved cold and heat, hunger and loneliness, death and deprivation as t hey planted firmly those wonderful country churches which had so joyously filled my lifetime. The frontiers of today's circuit rider have new names . . . drugs, crime, violence, illiteracy, poverty, rejection, liberation theology, humanism. With all the baggage of fringe benefits and status and security out of my saddlebag, I had been free to travel light and easy with nothing but God's Word and his eternal promises. Those have not changed. America could indeed take hope. It is not too late, but it is the zero hour.

Bishop Hunt had been right, this story must be told, for it is not my story, it is the story of hundreds of faithful saints in the hundreds of growing evangelical churches of America who are all proving that it can happen anywhere. Hallelujah!

I descended each of those pulpits with enormous optimism and gratitude. Indeed, all things do work together for good to them that love him. Like Job, when he forgave his friends his end was indeed better than his beginning. Over and over from each pulpit I seemed to hear Oscar's clear, deep, rich bass echoing his favorite prayer to his adoped land: "My country, 'tis of thee, sweet land of liberty, of thee I sing . . . long may our land be bright with freedom's holy light; protect us by the might, great God our King."

Soon the five weeks were gone. It was good to be back home with a new perspective. Florida, cool, lush and rain-drenched, welcomed us back.

Was there beneath the discord in the United Methodist Church a stream of God's people led by his Holy Spirit with a volume a thousand times greater than those destroying the church?

Without pastoral leadership, all on their own, as their surprise to me, the Trilby youth and laity had packed the church for a five-day day camp while we were gone. They had packed the church to capacity. Many had accepted Christ. It was the best gift they had ever given me. Now I knew we had truly mature Christians at the helm and that this was the secret of church growth.

And, our singles had also flourished. Two members of that group, Steve and Jan, had found God's will for their lives. Steve, with a turbulent youth and prison behind him, was now successful in his own business. Jan, with God's help, had struggled to raise her family alone. Now both her children were officers in the vibrant youth group. They had waited for me to return so I could marry them. A simple ceremony on a Saturday night was all they felt their broken, healed lives merited.

"Do you know for certain your sins are forgiven? Is your life new in Christ?" I asked them.

When I heard their resounding affirmation, I said, "Then even the bishop could bless your marriage. I will ask him to help me perform the ceremony when he comes in two weeks."

I called Bishop Hunt, and he arranged a meeting with Judy Kavenaugh, former Florida state attorney and close friend Quillian Yancy, himself, Jim and me for the next week.

In preparation for that meeting, a call to Bob Kohler, a director for the Division of Ordained Ministries of the General Board of Higher Education and Ministry in Nashville, produced the answers I sought. "There is no possibility of playing their game if they use defective procedures. There is a very personal and institutional bias toward women. Votes are probably counted before you go in, so it is a kiss of death. I was aware of your case. The Registrar of the Florida BOM called me about you. . . . The only thing we talked about was time requirement. To me, time in any conference is time served. Full time is time you have no other employment, and you have five such years in Florida, eight in Missouri. Florida has now sought to make a local rule, which they do not presently have, which would say all four years must be done in Florida. They are going to arbitrarily call your first two years supply, thus you cannot meet with the Board for two more years."

With a new rule they could retire me before even those two years could be counted. "It seems to me you have served a lifetime in the United Methodist Church," he continued, "Two years served as part-time clergy now equal a whole year credit, so you have served twelve years as clergy and twelve as a professor. By the Florida BOM's arithmetic that adds up to only two years.

"There is no question you had conference membership in 1973. The pension board should give you annuity for the years served. I would protest both that and the CPE."

I called the hospital chaplain, who wrote a letter to the BOM stating that his course was designed for freshmen students in an unaccredited seminary, not for someone with a doctorate in the field.

Before the meeting, Judy, Quillian and Bishop Hunt all received a copy of the then unfinished manuscript for this book. We met in the bishop's beautiful conference room. They had all read it. Bishop Hunt said he sat up all night reading it and had not refuted a single statement. His words were, "Print it. It's a best seller."

The bishop began. He said that he felt certain I had membership, but that the records might have been lost or recorded incorrectly, or the questions asked to everyone but me. Missouri should correct that.

"Even so, you have met the requirements again and again, both in Missouri and in Florida. If you hadn't I would never have called the Florida Board to meet with you this spring."

We parted friends. His only promise was that he would try to advocate the next few days while he was in office. Perhaps it could be brought up at Pastor's School next fall, or I could try again next year (an impossibility since then the new rule would prevent it). Judy felt we had exhausted Matthew 18:14-18 and that we should seek help outside the church. I had struggled with that issue but had resolved it by reading 1 Corinthians 6:6-7:

> . . . one brother goes to law against another—and this in front of unbelievers! The very fact that you have lawsuits among you means you have been completely defeated already. Why not rather be wronged? Why not rather be cheated?

I had advocated as far as I could for my voiceless brothers and sisters. I had pinpointed some of the reasons they were excluded, and why the church was dying. Now it was up to the laity. I would not take the church to court.

Many United Methodist pastors with guaranteed conference membership have not been able to do what their predecessors standing alone on a raw-boned American frontier did with nothing but a sure call and a Bible in their hands. (The core reason for the decline of the United Methodist Church is that we have neglected to believe and preach the Word.) God had done research, and my lack of membership was a part of the study . . . a part of his plan. Bishop and Mrs. Hunt invited us to have dinner with them. Over fellowship and a gracious meal, I asked Methodism's leading bishop the crucial question I had never allowed myself to ask:

"Bishop, will there always be a Methodist church?"

Without hesitation, but with great sadness, he replied, "There will always be a Methodist church. *There may not always be a United Methodist Church."*

I could hardly believe my ears. It was a conclusion he had reached long before I had dared ask the question.

Bishop Hunt was laying down the reigns after a lifetime of service to the United Methodist Church. The UM bishops honored him by electing him p resident of the Council of Bishop. Yet, tragically, during our twenty-fourth year of decline he presided over the greatest loss in Methodist history—seventy thousand members *lost.* Out there in the murky, storm-filled days and nights lay America at the Point of No Return. At every crossroad lay the multitude of wounded souls lost "beside the road" while Methodists passed by on the other side . . . seventy thousand laypersons had left the church, not to mention the thousands of lost people who might be won if Wesley's message and the new United Methodist Theological Statement rang from every pulpit. Other Protestants have had even longer funeral processions. (Half of all Baptist churches do not have even one baptism a year.) Other churches have experienced splits and scandals eroding their strength.

If we needed a second opinion, Bishop Emerson Colaw (who retired the same time as Bishop Hunt) observed in the September 30, 1988 *United Methodist Reporter*:

> Pastors who have never been part of a growing denomination and don't believe it is God's will for the church to grow are ringing the death knell for local United Methodist congregations. I've come to the conclusion that too many Methodist ministers accept the denomination's membership decline as normal.

No wonder such ministers and the Board of Ministry guarded jealously the appointments that were left. It did not take a mathematician to calculate the years until, at this rate, the bishop's prediction would be reality.

But this is not just a matter of statistics. Each church lost is a precious unpainted, rusty tin-roofed pioneer dream or a high steeple-stained glass historic pulpit abandoned on the altar of liberal theology, lost visions, lulled-to-sleep laity. Each member is an enormously precious soul who will spend an eternity in either heaven or hell.

Each Methodist church has the identical heritage, the identical "*Offer Them Christ*" dream Wesley engraved on Methodism and which pastors of growing churches still find effective.

It was incredible that the bishop said, "There may not always be a United Methodist Church." For this he and Oscar and I and countless clergy and laity, had given our lives to preserve. God would never be without his witness, but would it be in the United Methodist Church? Indeed, could not my journey have been in many other declining denominations as well?

Meanwhile, the world was a ticking time bomb. While the population had tripled, Methodists were in their twenty-fourth year of decline.

The morning paper read,

> In the next 30 minutes, 285 children will become victims of broken homes, 685 teenagers will take some form of narcotics and 57 kids will become runaways. The incident of divorce in the U.S. will likely remain the highest in the world (1986 Census Bureau Predictions). Of the 3.6 million U.S. children who began their formal school in the US last September, 14% were born to unmarried parents; 40% will live in broken homes before they reach the age of 18; as many as one-third are latchkey children with no one to greet them when they come home from school. Some 100,000 of America's children are homeless on any given night, and that doesn't include those who have run away from home or been kicked out by their parents. The National Academy of Sciences—not the church—called it a "national disgrace that must be treated with urgency that such a situation demands" (Don McCrory, *Eternity*, June 1987).

Drug and alcohol addiction were destroying the genes of the next generation. Our prisons were overcrowded, our welfare rolls swelling, our cities a jungle of crime. And all this had happened while I was a pastor. I had let it happen.

Science and technology declared that the greenhouse effect made the summer of 1988 the most torrid, drought-ridden summer in the history of the world. *Time* magazine did a cover story on the insane pollution in our oceans and streams and the terror of polluted earth and skies. We were destroying this earth because we had no hope of another. Indeed, it seemed God's controversy with America had begun in earnest.

Christians everywhere were predicting the Second Coming. Dates were set and books were written. To some it meant a time to speed up witness, to others a cop out. Perhaps our demise will be a more gradual one, allowing us time to look at the consequences. Regardless of how it happens, there is no question this is the day to be shouting from the housetops, "It can happen anywhere and must happen everywhere," a time for an Evangelism Explosion.

"God is dead" and liberation theology and liberal social gospel had left our land, our people, our churches devoid of Jesus Christ, the *only* Hope of the World. United Methodists have had the answer all along. Jesus said, "I am the way, the Truth and the Life." But we wanted our own way, replacing God's wisdom with man's. Nevertheless, the hammers of disbelief have not altered the anvil of his Word.

History has taught us that America was founded on a covenant. When God enters into a covenant it is forever. We, especially the United Methodist Church, have betrayed that covenant, and it is small wonder that we are threatened with extinction.

But there is hope. If Methodists would return to the Book they would see the answer in 2 Chronicles 7:14:

> If my people, who are called by my name, will humble themselves and pray and seek my face and turn from their wicked ways, then will I hear from heaven and will forgive their sin and will heal their land.

Nineveh, though at the brink of disaster, listened to the reluctant prophet, Jonah, and was spared. Washington, with his prayers and wisdom, preserved a nation. Lincoln and a little lady named Harriet Beecher Stowe turned the tide of slavery. Hundreds of people symbolically joined the one woman who refused to sit in the back of the bus. Powerful forces for right and justice are at work within the

United Methodist Church. What if we really meant the new theological statement and demanded that Wesley's theology really became that of the United Methodist Church? What if we defined the purpose of the church as outlined in the Scripture? What if soul winning and making disciples were the criteria used when pastors are evaluated? What if lay persons held the key to entrance into the United Methodist pulpit, the Episcopacy and administrative offices of our church?

What if those concerned with the demise of the United Methodist Church stormed the General Conference with petitions demanding these measures before it is too late? (And made sure that their legal petitions were heard!) What if that began now and next year we could see seven thousand churches rise out of nothingness and seventy thousand Methodists born again?

We need to select clergy, not in some one-night stand before a Board of Ministry, but as corporations do, by evaluating their effectiveness and loyalty to the aims and goals of the head of our church, Jesus Christ.

We are selling the Water of Life to a world which is gasping for it, drying up and dying right before our very eyes for lack of it. This is a crisis time, a matter of life or death.

Ezekiel 33:8 says,

> When I say to the wicked, 'O wicked man, you will surely die,' and you do not speak out to dissuade him from his ways, that wicked man will die for his sin, and I will hold you accountable for his blood.

God will be holding us responsible. Better to have the reckoning day here and now, before there is no United Methodist Church.

It would take time and great determination by the laity to implement such a plan. While waiting for that to happen, we cannot sit on our hands. Hundreds of dedicated Christians—men, women, old and young—could revive and build churches on faith. Hundreds of evangelical United Methodist churches could adopt the revitalization of Methodism as their mission and send out their best called layperson to make it happen. If each such church would send their best laypersons on a mission to revive a dead church, the home church would soon gain a new vision which would replace those lost to missions. It might be the most adrenalin-pumping project your church has ever tried. If done on a large scale, it could turn our decline to victory!

The Five Year Course of Study provides for lay persons in second careers to take courses each summer to become approved as lay pastors. Hundreds of dedicated laypersons trained as lay pastors could revive dying churches. Many of these persons have skills, experience and degrees, maturity, security and years of insights gained as lay persons working in the church. They are a source yet untapped.

It is not hard to get appointed to a closed church. Any D.S. would gladly do it. Where would the world have been if the early disciples of Jesus waited for conference membership or the General Conference to act? Travel America's highways and you will see hundreds of empty churches . . . high steeple and low steeple . . . gasping for breath. But by the Holy Spirit's guidance, they could breathe again. The purpose of this book is to say that even without membership, salary, prestige or parsonage, with nothing but God's eternal promises, it can happen anywhere in any denomination.

This will require reborn leaders who love the church, who believe Luke 9:23: "If anyone would come after me, he must deny himself and take up his cross daily and follow me."

Too many United Methodists think they are doing that right now and that it demands no price. But those who are world changers must pay any price, go any place, seek no reward but his final "Well done." It means an unconditional surrender to God's will, to the everlasting covenant God has made for our land. Just as it did for the early disciples, it may mean death or martyrdom. We have few choices. We will either build a fire or be consumed by fire.

On August 21, 1988, Bishop Hunt said his final farewell to Florida from Trilby's pulpit. It was an enormous honor to hear the final sermon of his active episcopacy. The newspaper headlines read "President of United Methodist Council of Bishops Returns to His Roots, the Little Country Church, to Preach His Final Sermon."

A gentle rain falling all Saturday night had lulled us to sleep. The August Sunday morning dawned clear, cool and crisp. Trilby church was sparkling, shiny as a new penny. Every nook and cranny was aglow with the Holy Spirit's newness as well as fresh garden flowers. The old bell from the "Blue Bell Bar" rang a strong and sure welcome. Norm's triumphant trumpet carried the lead for the piano and organ and a choir loft filled with those to whom God had given a new song: "Victory in Jesus."

This day belonged to the bishop and the laity. We would seek to bring him back home where he began, to let him see the power and possibility of a well trained evangelical laity, to give him a vision to carry to all Methodists that hope is not dead.

Together we sang the songs the congregation chose, broke the bread, shared each other's laughter, warmth, and pilgrim journey. Laity led the worship. Bill told the children's story; the youth manned their puppets. The children lit the candles and presented Bishop and Mrs. Hunt with an engraved plaque that read "World's Top Banana."

We had invited old friends from the bishop's childhood days in Johnson City, Tennessee. Their nostalgia opened the floodgates of warmth and memory. Earl Hunt had moved to the other side of the tracks. There he and Mary Ann met in fifth grade at Wilder Elementary school. He was always sweet on her, she was such a cute little thing, but she had to be persuaded.

Mrs. Love, who had gone to high school with them, invaded the worship, dressed in a 1930s depression era get-up. She was hilarious and the great bishop and his wife recalled her involvement in the warm and wonderful courtship days which led to a love that had lasted forty-five years.

The bishop may have traveled around the world and to the top of the ladder of Methodism, but today, in the luxury of a new born country church set amid sordid poverty, for this day and this hour he was back home. For today, there was no dying United Methodist Church, no declining statistics, no closed churches, no heartbreak.

As he dedicated the magnificent precast concrete building and the Rose Room, he affirmed again what the Board of Ministry had rejected. "I was here four years ago and preached where we ate our dinner. Now I have come back and seen not one miracle but a series of miracles that have been wrought here.

"You have to see it to believe it. No way can you go out and tell people about it. Oh, you can do it but they will look at you like you ought to see a psychiatrist. They say you just don't understand. Well, you really don't understand because what happened here couldn't happen here. Oh, it did, but it couldn't.

"It happened because whenever the church of the Lord Jesus

Christ is turned loose in a community to help human beings and meet their needs and lift up the name of Jesus Christ, that church becomes indispensable in the community.

"The problem of church growth is a very simple problem. The only thing we have to do to get the church to grow is to help the church do more of what it is supposed to be doing all along. That is exactly what happened here. . . . "

Now it was time for the sermon everyone had come to hear. He had called earlier in the week to ask me to suggest a sermon topic. In answer, I told him what I had waited for seventeen years for some Board of Ministry to say to me: "Just tell how you accepted Christ, what he means to you, and how others can know for certain they have eternal life."

He read from Hebrew 12:22-23: "But you have come to Mount Zion, to the heavenly Jerusalem, the city of the living God. You have come to thousands upon thousands of angels in joyful assembly, to the church of the firstborn, whose names are written in heaven. You have come to God, the judge of all men, to the spirits of righteous men made perfect."

"In my first church there was a woman who would never come to church," Bishop Hunt continued, "but finally on my last Sunday she came. She sat in the front row and left early. As we were seated around the parsonage table the phone rang and she gave me the finest theory on public worship I had ever heard. She said, 'Because I went to church today, the beans tasted better.' When you worship together, even the beans taste better."

He affirmed that when we come to church we come to a *spiritual fellowship*. At church, people think about values and principles that are unseen. We have lost that capacity in our world today. We have to have it all written down where we can touch and handle it. But that is not God's way. Those things that we never can write down and never can put out where we can see them are the real things that constitute the meaning of life. The church is the place where we think about those things.

Church is also the place of a *universal fellowship*. We come to a place where we forget if we are rich or poor, whether we have been to school or haven't, forget the color of our skin, what language we speak, how important or unimportant we are in the community.

We come to an *immortal fellowship*. In Europe they keep two rolls of church members, those who belong to the church still militant and those in the church triumphant. I felt an overwhelming oneness with those I have loved and lost awhile.

He was closing his message and his ministry by emphasizing his final point with staccato: "When you come to church, you come to a *redemptive fellowship*. You come to the blood of sprinkling."

That great, towering bishop was no longer old and retiring; he was a boy again. It was Saturday and the family had gone away visiting. All alone at home, kneeling beside his bed, he asked Christ into his life, just as his Methodist Sunday school teacher had taught him he could do. He came, as each of us must come, as Wesley had come at Aldersgate, accepting Christ and Christ alone for salvation.

> Over these many years in one church and the other I have seen that those who accept him find that miracles happen. They come to him old and tired and leave refreshed. They come guilty and leave forgiven, they come out-of-heart and out-of-hope and leave with a song in their hearts and the morning star rising above them.

He was through . . . but as an afterthought, a final punctuation to all that his ministry and the church had meant to him, he turned back to the pulpit once more. It was his final message to the dying United Methodist Church. "There is a sign that should be hung over every church door. It should read, *broken lives mended here*. Truly that is what has happened at Trilby."

Now the organ and trumpet were sounding the triumphant wedding march. Steve and Jan, whose lives had once been broken but were mended at this very altar, came forward to the eternal strains of Lohengrin. There they stood, forgiven, redeemed disciples confessing their love before the ancient Bible on the recycled altar fragrant with roses picked in the prayer garden's morning dew.

As they repeated to each other and to God their eternal vows, the bishop blessed the rings, declared them one and reached for my hand as we both laid on them God's hand of blessing.

The brilliant late afternoon sun shone its golden rays through the window with the shepherd cradling the wounded lamb.

As they rose and were pronounced one in Christ, those two, born again, lives renewed, sins forgiven, their kids in tow, confidently marched out to face the future with Christ in their hearts.

The silver trumpet and the mighty organ heralded the triumphant strains of Handel's *Hallelujah Chorus,* bringing that victorious country congregation to its feet. In one united voice, young and old, rich and poor, bishop and clergy, all broke into joyous song and thunderous applause.

Perhaps the applause was so spontaneous and enthusiastic, the singing so triumphant, the emotion so down home, country church genuine, the message so imperative, the occasion so memorably historic that few heard the great bishop silently laying down his well-worn reins.

Comments and responses to the material in this book are welcome. Please address correspondence to Rose Grindheim Sims, Box 631, Dade City, Florida 33525. Telephone: 904/567-6065.

Dr. Rose Sims was again denied membership at the 1989 session of the Florida Annual Conference, despite a written protest from the Trilby Administrative Board and a request by Dr. Sims that the Florida Board of Ordained Ministry reconsider her case.

In the meantime Trilby was recognized at the 1989 Annual Conference session for leading the conference again in professions of faith for churches of 101-250 members. Trilby completed and dedicated a new education unit and has purchased a lot for more parking and possibly a new parsonage. Dr. Rose said, "We have just finished the best year we've ever had at Trilby. We are more convinced than ever that what happened here ***can happen anywhere*** *if we only honor God's Word and are faithful."*

September 1989